Bloopers,
BLUNDERS,
Jokes,
QUIPS
&
"Quotes"

Bloopers
BLUNDERS
Jokes
QUIPS
& "Quotes"

Compiled
by

Jim Kraus

Tyndale House Publishers, Inc., Carol Stream, Illinois

Visit Tyndale online at www.tyndale.com.

TYNDALE and Tyndale's quill logo are registered trademarks of Tyndale
House Publishers, Inc.

Bloopers, Blunders, Jokes, Quips & "Quotes" © 2005 by Tyndale House
Publishers. All rights reserved.

Text compiled by Jim Kraus

Designed and illustrated by Luke Daab

Edited by Bonne Steffen

Scripture quotations are taken from the *Holy Bible,* New Living Translation,
copyright © 1996, 2004 by Tyndale House Foundation. Used by permission
of Tyndale House Publishers, Inc., Carol Stream, Illinois 60188. All rights
reserved.

ISBN 978-1-4143-0547-9

Printed in the United States of America

16   15   14   13   12   11
10   9   8   7   6   5

A Beginning Thought . . .

or Two . . .

or Three

Somewhere I have read that medical research has discovered that the act of laughing increases the body's ability to fight off disease and actually helps the body heal itself from serious illnesses. I think it was in some well-respected medical journal. If not, well, it should have been.

–JIM KRAUS

For the happy heart, life is a continual feast.
PROVERBS 15:15

A cheerful heart is good medicine.
PROVERBS 17:22

BLOOPER

We must be kind to strangers because we may be entertaining angels in their underwear.

Quote

We are inclined to believe those we don't know—
because, after all, they've never lied to us before.

JOKE

A woman decided to have her portrait painted. She told the artist, "Paint me with diamond rings, a diamond necklace, diamond bracelets, a diamond brooch, and a diamond-encrusted gold Rolex."

"But you're not wearing any of those things," he replied.

"I know," she said. "It's in case I should die before my husband. I'm sure he'll remarry right away, and I want his new wife to go crazy looking for the jewelry."

2

BLOOPER

To raise money for their missions trip, the St. James youth group is smelling cookbooks. Bring your cash or checks to the Sunday service and see a young person.

Quote

Nobody forgets where the hatchet is buried.

JOKE

Christmas break was over and the teacher was asking the class about their vacations. She turned to one boy and asked him what he did over the break.

"We visited my grandmother in Punxsutawney, Pennsylvania," he replied.

"That sounds like an excellent spelling word," the teacher said. "Can you tell the class how you spell that?"

Without hesitating, he said, "You know, come to think of it, we went to New York City."

3

Quote

If you got everything you wanted, where would you put it?

JOKE

A fellow is shipwrecked. When he wakes up, he's on a beach. The sand is dark red. He can't believe it. The sky is dark red. He walks around a bit and sees dark red grass, dark red birds, and dark red fruit on the dark red trees. He's shocked when he realizes that his skin is turning dark red, too.

"Oh, no!" he says. "I've been marooned!"

4

BLOOPER

Bride Cindy Fox wore a lovely lace veil that fell to the floor as she walked down the aisle.

Quote

A team effort is a lot of people doing what I say.

JOKE

The world's first fully computerized airliner was ready for its maiden flight without pilots or crew. The plane taxied to the loading area automatically, its doors opened automatically, the steps came out automatically. The passengers boarded the plane and took their seats.

The steps retracted automatically, the doors closed automatically, and the airplane taxied toward the runway. Everything happened without a hitch.

As the passengers leaned back in their comfortable seats, a voice came over the intercom. "Good afternoon, ladies and gentlemen. Welcome to the debut of the world's first fully computerized airliner. Everything on this aircraft is run electronically. We're cruising at 35,000 feet. Just sit back and relax. Nothing can go wrong. . . . Nothing can go wrong. . . . Nothing can go wrong. . . ."

5

Have You Heard the One about . . .

A huge football fan receives a free ticket to the Super Bowl from his company. Unfortunately, when he arrives at the stadium he realizes the seat is in the last row in the corner of the stadium—he is closer to the Goodyear Blimp than the field.

About halfway through the first quarter, the fan notices an empty seat 10 rows off the field on the 50-yard line. He decides to take a chance and makes his way through the stadium to the empty seat.

Before he sits down, he taps the shoulder of the man in the next seat over. "Excuse me, is anyone sitting here?" The man says no. The fan can't keep his excitement to himself. He turns to the man and says, "This is incredible! Who in their right mind would buy a seat like this at the Super Bowl and not use it?"

"Well, actually the seat belongs to me," the man replies. "I was supposed to come with my wife, but she passed away. This is the first Super Bowl we haven't attended together since we got married in 1967."

"That's really sad," says the fan. "Couldn't you find a relative or a close friend to take the seat?"

"No," the man replies, "they're all at the funeral."

6

BLOOPER

On a sign at St. Michael's Church in Herrid, South Dakota, during a cold spell: "Many are cold, but few are chosen."

Quote

It would have made our lives easier if the pioneers had located cities closer to the airports.

JOKE

Dining out one evening, a man noticed 6 teenagers boisterously celebrating an event at a nearby table. Toward the end of their meal, one of them pulled out a camera.

"Hey, wait a minute," one of her companions said. "You have to be in the picture too."

The man asked if he could help, much to the delight of the camera owner. He snapped a picture of the group, but not being completely familiar with the camera, the man said, "Do you want me to take another picture in case that one doesn't come out?"

"Oh, no, that's OK," the teen replied. "I always get double prints."

7

BLOOPER

A 7-pound baby boy, Thomas Gavin, arrived last night to frighten the lives of Sherman and Edie Forrest.

Quote

Never wrestle with a pig. You get dirty; and besides, the pig enjoys it.

JOKES

Q: What do you get if you cross a four-leaf clover with poison oak?

A: A rash of good luck.

Q: What do you get when you cross a pillowcase with a stone?

A: A Sham rock.

Q: Why should you never iron a four-leaf clover?

A: You don't want to press your luck.

8

BLOOPER

All food left in the church kitchen refrigerators must be removed on Friday for cleaning.

Quote

Happiness is getting a bill you've already paid, which means you can sit down and write a nasty letter.

JOKE

The CEO was scheduled to speak at an important convention, so he asked his assistant to write him a punchy 20-minute speech.

When the CEO returned from the big event, he was furious.

Cornering his assistant, he didn't hold back. "What's the idea of writing me an hour-long speech?! Half the audience walked out before I finished."

"I wrote you a 20-minute speech," the assistant replied, baffled. "And I also gave you the 2 extra copies you requested."

9

BLOOPER

John Ringhofer, head of city maintenance, reminds everyone in church that city residents can drop off trees at any time.

Quote

Some people pay a compliment as if they wanted a receipt.

JOKE

A man walks into a coat-and-tie-only restaurant and asks to be seated. The waiter says, "Sir, you don't have a coat or a tie."

So the man goes out to his truck and gets a jacket. When he comes back in, he asks, "May I be seated?"

The waiter replies, "Sir, you don't have a tie."

So the man goes back out to his truck and wraps jumper cords around his neck. He comes back in and says, "Now may I be seated?"

The waiter says, "OK, but don't go trying to start something."

10

Part 1

Things My Mama Taught Me

My mama taught me to appreciate **a job well done.**
If you're going kill each other, do it outside. I just finished cleaning!

My mama taught me **religion.**
You'd better pray that will come out of the carpet.

My mama taught me about **time travel.**
If you don't straighten up, I'm going to knock you into the middle of next week!

My mama taught me **logic.**
Because I said so, that's why.

My mama taught me **advanced logic.**
If you fall out of that swing and break your neck, you're not going to the store with me.

My mama taught me **foresight.**
Make sure you wear clean underwear, in case you're in an accident.

My mama taught me **irony.**
Keep crying, and I'll give you something to really cry about.

11

BLOOPER

10:30 a.m. worship service and candle lighting in remembrance of those who have died during the previous year at both worship services.

Quote

I like long walks, especially when they are taken by people who annoy me.

JOKE

A tour bus full of noisy tourists arrived at Runnymede, England. They gathered around the guide, who said, "This is the spot where the barons forced King John to sign the Magna Carta."

A man pushing his way to the front of the crowd asked, "When did that happen?"

"1215," answered the guide.

The man looked at his watch and said, "Rats! Just missed it by half an hour!"

12

BLOOPER

Correction: In last Sunday's bulletin, the outline on budgeting personal income read: Spend 80%, Save 20%, Tithe 10%. It should be: Spend 80%, Save 15%, Tithe 10%.

Quote

Having a big family is a good way to make sure there will always be someone to answer the phone—and forget the message.

JOKES

Q: What do you call a boomerang that doesn't work?
A: A crooked stick.

Q: What do you call cheese that isn't yours?
A: Nacho cheese.

Q: What do you call 4 bullfighters in quicksand?
A: Quatro sinko.

13

Quote

It is possible to come back from Las Vegas with a small fortune—providing you went there with a large one.

JOKE

A man went to his pastor with a burning question. "Pastor, is it proper for one man to profit from another man's mistakes?"

"No, a man should not profit from another man's mistakes," answered the pastor.

"Are you sure, Pastor?"

"Of course, I'm sure. In fact, I'm positive," the pastor replied.

"OK, Pastor, how about returning the $200 I gave you for marrying me!"

14

BLOOPER

Church newsletter classifieds: For sale—Snow blower.
Five horsepower. Worked fine last summer.

Quote

A hypochondriac can't leave being well enough alone.

JOKE

Three older ladies were discussing the travails of aging.
One said, "Sometimes I catch myself in front of the
refrigerator with a jar of mustard in my hand and can't
remember whether I need to put it away or start making
a sandwich."

The 2nd lady chimed in, "Yes, sometimes I find myself
on the stairs and can't remember whether I was on my
way up or on my way down."

The 3rd one responded while rapping her knuckles on
the table. "Well, I'm glad I don't have that problem; knock
on wood."

Then she said, "Wait, someone must be at the door;
I'll get it!"

15

It Takes Years to Learn that . . .

* there is a very fine line between "hobby" and "mental illness."

* you never lick a steak knife.

* it's important to take out the fortune before you eat the cookie.

* you should never say anything to a woman that even remotely suggests that you think she's pregnant unless you can see an actual baby emerging from her at that moment.

* the one thing that unites all human beings (regardless of age, gender, religion, economic status, or ethnic background) is that deep down inside, we *all* believe that we are above-average drivers.

* the main accomplishment of almost all organized protests is to annoy people who are not in them.

* you must never be afraid to try something new. Remember that a lone amateur built the ark; a large group of professionals built the Titanic.

16

Quote

To improve your memory,
lend people money.

JOKE

As a jet was flying over Arizona on a clear day, the pilot was giving a running commentary about landmarks over the public address system.

"Coming up on the right, you can see the Meteor Crater, which is a major tourist attraction in northern Arizona. It was formed when a lump of nickel and iron, roughly 150 feet in diameter and weighing 300,000 tons, struck the earth at about 40,000 miles an hour, scattering white-hot debris for miles in every direction. The hole measures nearly a mile across and is about 550 feet deep."

From the cabin, a passenger exclaimed, "Wow! It just missed the highway!"

17

BLOOPER

Fire chief Andrew Lloyd reminds the congregation to call 911 if they smell gas. He says that you can stop a gas leak with one finger.

Quote

No one is so old that he thinks he cannot live one more year.

JOKE

Caller to the IRS: I want to know if I should file married or single.
IRS: Are you married?
Caller: Well, sort of . . .
IRS: What?
Caller: Well, we did get married, but we're not counting on it to last all that long.

18

BLOOPER

The Seaview homeschooling parent group is looking for an English tooter for several of their high school students.

Quote

Opera is when a guy gets stabbed in the back and instead of bleeding, he sings.

JOKES

Eye-catching signs:

In a dry cleaner's window: Those leaving their garments here for more than 30 days will be disposed of.

Outside a muffler shop: No appointment necessary. We hear you coming.

Spotted in a safari park: Elephants Please Stay In Your Car.

Notice posted on a fence: The farmer allows walkers to cross the field for free, but the bull charges.

BLOOPER

Rent-a-Senior Fund-Raiser: "We'll clean your house for you. Why risk a poor quality cleaning job when we guarantee it?"

Quote

Most people can keep a secret. It's the people they tell who can't.

JOKE

Expecting their 2nd child, a couple attended a pre-birth class specifically for those who had already had at least one child. The instructor raised the issue of breaking the news to the older child. It went like this:

"Some parents," she said, "tell the older child, 'We love you so much we decided to bring another child into this family.' But think about that. Ladies, what if your husband came home one day and said, 'Honey, I love you so much I decided to bring home another wife'?"

To which one of the female class members answered, "Does she cook?"

20

Part 1

Manly Men Never Say . . .

* Do you think my gut is too big?
* I'll have fruit instead of biscuits and gravy.
* Honey, we don't need another dog.
* Give me the small bag of pork rinds.
* Too many deer heads detract from the decor.
* Trim the fat off that steak.
* Cappuccino tastes better than espresso.
* The tires on that truck are too big.
* I'll have the *arugula* and *radicchio* salad.
* Little Debbie snack cakes have too many fat grams.
* Here's a *Hee Haw* episode that we haven't seen.
* I would like the salad dressing on the side, please.

BLOOPER

Out to lunch. If not back by 5, out for dinner also.

Quote

Never forget that you are part of the people who
can be fooled part of the time.

JOKE

One rainy evening, a husband and wife emerged from a
restaurant only to find that the husband had locked the
keys in the car. He insisted he could open the door with a
wire coat hanger, so he went back to the restaurant to get
one. There were none to be found.

He then ran to a dry cleaners four blocks away and
returned with a hanger. After a few attempts, he got the
door open and the couple climbed in. As he sat there,
soaked and cold, the husband stuck the hanger under his
seat. With a smug grin, he said, "Now if this ever happens
again, I'll be prepared."

22

BLOOPER

Faith is 90 percent spiritual. The other half is not.

Quote

The truly thoughtful teenager leaves enough gas in the car so you can make it to the gas station.

JOKES

Q: What type of lettuce was served on the Titanic?
A: Iceberg.

Q: What lies at the bottom of the ocean and twitches?
A: A nervous wreck.

Q: Where do you find a dog with no legs?
A: Right where you left him.

Q: Why are there so many Smiths in the phone book?
A: They all have phones.

23

Quote

When he put his 2 cents worth in, at least he wasn't overcharging.

JOKE

A kindergarten class went on a field trip to their local police station.

Tacked up on the bulletin board in the squad room, the kids saw a group of photos labeled "The 10 Most Wanted."

One of the youngsters pointed to a mug shot and asked if it really was the photo of a criminal.

"Yes," said the policeman, "the detectives want him very badly."

"Then why didn't you keep him when you took his picture?"

24

Elders are discussing methods to fix future church elections.

Quote

Horse sense is what keeps horses from betting on what people will do.

JOKE

A minister was visiting a 95-year-old church member at the nursing home.

"How are you feeling?" the pastor asked.

"I'm just worried sick!" the woman replied.

"What are you worried about, dear?" the clergyman asked. "You're getting good care, aren't you?"

"Yes, they are taking very good care of me."

"Are you in any pain?"

"Just a little arthritis."

"So what's the matter?" her pastor asked.

The lady leaned forward in her rocking chair. "Every close friend I ever had has already died and gone to heaven. I'm afraid they're all wondering where *I* went."

25

Part 2
Things My Mama Taught Me

My mama taught me about the science of **osmosis.**
Shut your mouth and eat your supper!

My mama taught me about **contortionism.**
Will you "look" at the dirt on the back of your neck!

My mama taught me about **stamina.**
You'll sit there 'til every bit of that spinach is gone.

My mama taught me about **weather.**
It looks as if a tornado swept through your room.

My mama taught me how to solve **physics problems.**
*If I yelled because I saw a meteor coming toward you,
would you listen then?*

My mama taught me **the circle of life.**
I brought you into this world, and I can take you out.

My mama taught me **medical science.**
*If you don't stop crossing your eyes, they are going
to freeze that way.*

26

BLOOPER

Todd Besterly has two burial plots for sale. Great condition, slightly used.

Quote

People who say "nothing is impossible" don't have teenagers.

JOKE

It was the first day of school. Due to a staffing shortage, an elderly principal had been called out of retirement to fill in temporarily. As the principal made his rounds, he heard a terrible commotion in one of the classrooms.

He rushed in and spotted a tall boy who seemed to be making the most noise. Seizing the boy by the arm, the principal dragged him out in the hall, and told him to wait there until he was excused.

Returning to the classroom, the principal restored order and lectured the class for half an hour about the importance of good behavior.

"Now," he said, "are there any questions?"

"Please sir," one girl said timidly, "may we have our teacher back?"

BLOOPER

The Friday lunch at All Saints Day Care will be Mrs. Paul's dreaded fish sticks.

Quote

A husband who thinks he's smarter than his wife is married to a very smart woman.

JOKE

A woman had a wedding to attend and needed a wedding gift. *Aha,* she thought, *I have that monogrammed silver tray from my wedding that I never use. I'll just take it to a silversmith and have him remove my monogram and replace it with hers.* Voilà, *one cheap wedding present.*

She took it to the silversmith and gave him the instructions. After examining the tray carefully, the silversmith shook his head and said, "Lady, this can only be done so many times!"

28

BLOOPER

Morning sermon: Jesus Walks on Water.
Evening sermon: Searching for Jesus.

Quote

A practical nurse is one who marries a rich patient.

JOKE

An overweight fellow decided it was time to shed some excess pounds. He took his new diet seriously, even changing his driving route to avoid his favorite bakery. One morning, however, he arrived at work carrying a gigantic coffee cake. Everyone scolded him, but he had an explanation.

"This is a very special coffee cake," he said. "There was a detour so I had to drive by the bakery this morning. I felt this was no accident, so I prayed, 'Lord, if you want me to enjoy a delicious coffee cake with my coworkers, open up a parking place in front of the bakery.' "

"Sure enough," he said, "the 8th time around the block, there it was!"

BLOOPER

The singles group from the Somerton United Methodist Church welcomes singles of all ages who are widowed, divorced, or married.

Quote

Some people are good losers; the others can't act.

JOKE

A woman went to a computer dating service. During the interview, she said she didn't care about a man's looks, what kind of car he drove, what his income was, or his background. All she wanted was a man of upright character.

An hour later a man came in and told the matchmaker that the only thing he was seeking in a woman was intelligence. He didn't care about her looks or anything superficial.

The service matched them together immediately because they had one thing in common—they were both compulsive liars!

30

Part 1

As a College Freshman You Wish You'd Known . . .

* that it didn't matter how late you scheduled your first class because you'd sleep right through it;
* that chemistry labs require more time than all your other classes put together;
* that you can know everything and fail a test;
* that you can know nothing and ace a test;
* that you would be one of those people your parents warned you about;
* that resting on Sunday is a figment of the world's imagination;
* that psychology is really biology, biology is really chemistry, chemistry is really physics, and physics is really math.

31

BLOOPER

Seniors report: There will be no Seniors Alive in January.

Quote

Depend on the rabbit's foot, but remember—it didn't work for the rabbit.

JOKES

Intaxication: Euphoria at getting a tax refund, which lasts until you realize it was your money to start with.

Reintarnation: Coming back to life as a hillbilly.

Sarchasm: The gulf between the author of sarcastic wit and the person who doesn't get it.

Inoculatte: To take coffee intravenously when you are running late.

Hipatitis: Terminal coolness.

32

BLOOPER

Wanted: nanny for middle-aged boys.

Quote

Don't go into the water after a hearty meal.
You'll never find it there.

JOKE

An old preacher was dying. He requested that his IRS agent and his lawyer come to his home. When they entered his bedroom, the preacher motioned for them to sit on each side of the bed.

Both the IRS agent and lawyer were touched that the old preacher wanted them to be with him during his final moments. They were also curious, because the preacher had never particularly liked either one of them. Finally, the lawyer asked, "Pastor, why did you ask us to come?"

The old preacher mustered up some strength, then said weakly, "Jesus died between 2 thieves, and that's how I want to go too."

BLOOPER

The Petersons have a large English sheepdog ready for adoption. He's neutered like one of the family, and is very even-tempered.

Quote

I never repeat gossip, so listen the first time.

JOKE

One night, a torrential rain soaked southern Louisiana resulting in floodwaters about 6 feet high the next morning.

Mrs. Boudreaux was sitting on her roof with her neighbor, Mrs. Thibodaux, waiting for help.

Mrs. Thibodaux noticed a baseball cap floating near the house. It floated far out into the front yard, then all the way back to the house. It kept floating away and coming back.

Pointing, she asked Mrs. Boudreaux, "Do you see that baseball cap floating away from the house, then floating back again?"

"Oh," replied Mrs. Boudreaux, "that's Dewey. I told him he was going to cut the grass today come you-know-what or high water!"

34

BLOOPER

The council of elders at First Baptist of Richton Park will talk about the need for less talking at meetings.

Quote

Experience enables you to recognize
a mistake when you've made it again.

JOKE

A father took his sons, ages 7 and 5, to the park for a picnic. Before running to the playground apparatus, the 7-year-old read the posted playground rules to his brother.

"Don't jump on the merry-go-round when it's moving."
"Only go down the slide in a sitting position."
"One child on a swing at a time."

There were 10 rules, which the boys promised to obey.

After about a half hour of play, the father noticed the boys were obeying all the rules but one. They were coming down the slide headfirst!

When he pulled the boys aside to remind them of the posted rule, the 7-year-old replied, "Dad, don't be silly. No one uses the slide rule anymore!"

35

Phone Messages

* Hi. This is John. If you are the phone company,
  I already sent the money. If you are my parents,
  please send money. If you are my financial aid insti-
  tution, you didn't lend me enough money. If you are
  my friends, you owe me money. If you are a female,
  don't worry; I have plenty of money.

* Hi. John's answering machine is broken. This is the
  refrigerator. Please speak very slowly, and I'll stick
  your message to myself with one of these cute
  magnets.

* Hello, you are talking to a machine but I am capable
  of receiving messages. But first let me say: My owners
  do not need siding, windows, or a hot tub, and their
  carpets are clean. They give to charity through their
  office and do not need their picture taken. If you're
  still with me, leave your name and number, and they
  will get back to you.

* Hi. I am probably home. I'm just avoiding someone
  I don't like. Leave me a message, and if I don't call
  back, it's you.

BLOOPER

Pastor Fromme addressed the congregation concerning the new dress code for our youth group. The dress code includes no navels. They must be left at home, please.

Quote

I went on a 14-day diet, and all I lost was 2 weeks.

JOKE

A college freshman was 5 feet, 8 inches tall when he left for school in the fall. He worked through the Christmas holidays and didn't return home again until the February break.

When he got off the plane, his mother was startled at how much taller he looked. Getting the tape measure out at home, they discovered he had grown 3 inches! The student was as surprised as his mother. "Couldn't you tell by your clothes that you'd grown?" she asked him.

"Well, since I've been doing my own laundry," he replied, "I just figured everything had shrunk."

BLOOPER

Mr. and Mrs. Walsh named their new baby Julie Lynn after her aunt, Susan Marie Walsh.

Quote

If you miss your anniversary, you'll catch it later.

JOKE

A woman's husband died leaving her $20,000. After everything was settled with the funeral home and cemetery, she told her closest friend that all the money was gone.

"How can that be?" her friend asked. "You told me he had $20,000 when he died. How could you be broke already?"

"Well, the funeral cost me $7,000. And, of course, I had to give a donation to the church and the organist and all. That was $1,000, and I spent another $2,000 for the wake, food, and drinks. The rest went for the memorial stone."

The friend looked surprised. "You paid $10,000 for the stone? My goodness, how big was it?"

The widow answered, "Three carats!"

38

BLOOPER

We are rejoicing. The missing candlesticks were found by the tree behind the parking lot.

Quote

Don't worry about being average—you're as close to the top as you are to the bottom.

JOKE

It was mealtime during a flight to Chicago.

"Would you like dinner?" the flight attendant asked the passenger.

"What are my choices?" he asked.

"Yes or no," she replied.

BLOOPER

John Lister was at death's door—and the doctors and pastors pulled him through.

Quote

Interest your children in bowling—get them off the streets and into the alleys.

JOKE

Embroiled in a number of legal battles including a divorce, a man had become totally disgusted with lawyers in general. One evening at a restaurant counter, he began venting. "All lawyers are jerks," he loudly proclaimed.

A man sitting nearby immediately got up and confronted the complainer. "Look, I am highly offended by what you just said."

"Why? Are you a lawyer?" the man asked.

"No, I'm not. I'm a jerk!"

40

Travel Language

Tour Guide Says:	Translation:
Old world charm	No bath
Tropical	Rainy
Majestic setting	A long way from town
Options galore	Nothing is included in the itinerary
Secluded hideaway	Impossible to find or get to
Pre-registered rooms	Already occupied
Explore on your own	Pay for it yourself
Knowledgeable hosts	They've flown in an airplane before
No extra fees	No extras

BLOOPER

Correction: Master Technician Ross Lears of the U.S. Navy is not going to Mars as we mentioned in last Sunday's bulletin. He is going to Italy instead.

Quote

The best thing about dictating a letter is that you can use words that you don't know how to spell.

JOKE

Two friends were visiting Annapolis and noticed several plebes on their hands and knees in the courtyard with pencils and clipboards in hand. "What are they doing?" they asked a senior officer.

"Each year the freshmen are asked to determine how many bricks it took to finish paving this courtyard."

"So what's the answer?"

"One," he whispered.

42

BLOOPER

Betty Wilson found a large orange cat on Thursday. She says it is a female, affectionate, and nonsmoking.

Quote

English is a funny language. A fat chance and a slim chance are the same thing.

JOKE

The new librarian decided to change the book checkout procedure. Instead of writing the names of borrowers on the book cards herself, she asked the youngsters to sign their own names. "You are signing a contract instructing you to return the books on time," she explained.

A 2nd grader brought 4 books to the desk and gave the librarian his name. She, in turn, handed him the 4 book cards to sign. The boy, obviously disgusted, laboriously printed his name and handed them back to her.

Before the librarian could even start her speech he said, scornfully, "Our other librarian could write."

43

Quote

If it were not for marriage, husbands and wives would have to bicker with perfect strangers.

JOKE

Working as a computer instructor for an adult education program at a community college, I am keenly aware of the gap in computer knowledge between my younger and older students.

My observations were confirmed the day a new student walked into our library and glanced at the encyclopedia volumes on a bookshelf.

"What are all these books?" he asked.

"Encyclopedias," I answered, somewhat surprised.

"Really?" he said. "Someone printed out the whole thing?"

44

BLOOPER

Our speaker this evening will be Dr. Desters, who is a specialist in women and other diseases.

Quote

You think you have problems? We have a plumber who no longer makes house calls.

JOKE

A woman had finished shopping and exited the busy store at the same time as another woman did, equally loaded down with bags. The two of them looked around, trying to spot their cars in the crowded parking lot.

Just then the first woman's car horn beeped, and she pinpointed its location. Impressed, the second woman said, "I sure could use a gadget like that to help me find my car."

"Actually," the first replied, "that gadget is my husband."

45

Part 3
Things My Mama Taught Me

My mama taught me to **think ahead.**
If you don't pass your spelling test, you'll never get a good job.

My mama taught me **ESP.**
Put your sweater on; don't you think I know when you're cold?

My mama taught me **first aid.**
When that lawn mower cuts off your toes, don't come running to me.

My mama taught me how to become **an adult.**
If you don't eat your vegetables, you'll never grow up.

My mama taught me about **genetics.**
You're just like your father.

My mama taught me about my **roots.**
Do you think you were born in a barn?

46

Quote

Social tact is making your company feel at home, even though you wish they were.

JOKE

The local veterinarian in a small town in Maine was treating a vacationer's dog that had had an unfortunate encounter with a porcupine.

After prying, pulling, cutting, and stitching, he returned the dog to its owner.

"How much will that be?" the out-of-towner asked.

"A hundred dollars, ma'am," the vet answered.

"Why that's simply outrageous!" she stormed. "You're always trying to overcharge nonresidents. What do you do in the winter, when we're not here to be gypped?"

"Raise porcupines, ma'am."

47

BLOOPER

The church elders have hired a financial consultant at $500 a day to determine why the church has financial problems.

Quote

When it comes to work, there are many
who will stop at nothing.

JOKE

A nightclub owner hired a pianist and a drummer. After several performances, the owner discovered that the drummer had walked away with some of the club's valuables. He notified the police, and the drummer was arrested.

Desperate for another drummer, the owner called a friend who knew some musicians. "What happened to the drummer you had?" he asked the owner.

"I had him arrested," the owner replied.

There was a long pause. "How badly did he play?"

48

Quote

Where will I find the time not to read so many books?

JOKE

A man went to a drugstore to buy a hearing aid. "How
much does a hearing aid cost?" he asked the clerk.

"That depends," said the clerk. "Our hearing aids are
priced from $2.00 to $2,000."

"Let's see the $2 model," he said.

The clerk handed him the device. "You just stick this
button in your ear and run this cord down to your
pocket."

"How does it work?" the customer asked.

"It doesn't work," the clerk replied. "But when people
see it, they'll talk louder!"

49

BLOOPER

Brother Bill Amos is looking for volunteers to help point out his barn.

Quote

For most kids, cleanliness isn't next to godliness—it's next to impossible.

JOKE

A newly married man had only one complaint: His wife was always nursing sick birds. One winter evening, he found a raven with a splint on its wing sitting in his favorite chair. On the dining room table, instead of dinner, there was a feverish eagle pecking at an aspirin. In the kitchen, his wife was toweling down a shivering little wren she had found out in the snow.

Furious, the husband stormed out to the kitchen. "I can't take it anymore! We've got to get rid of these %$#@!! birds or—"

The wife held up her hand and cut him off in mid-sentence. "Please, no cuss words in front of the chilled wren."

50

Part 1

Funny Definitions

* **Antacid:** Uncle Acid's wife.
* **Arbitrator:** A cook that leaves Arby's to work at McDonald's.
* **Avoidable:** What a bullfighter tries to do.
* **Baloney:** Where some hemlines fall.
* **Bernadette:** The act of torching a mortgage.
* **Bottom:** What the shopper did when she found the shoes that she wanted.
* **Bucktooth:** The going rate for the tooth fairy.
* **Burglarize:** What a crook sees with.
* **Cantaloupe:** When you are unable to run away to get married.
* **Cartoonist:** What you call your auto mechanic.
* **Castanet:** What they did to fill the role of Frankie Avalon's movie girlfriend.
* **Celtics:** What a parasite salesman does.
* **Concerts:** Breath mints for inmates.

51

BLOOPER

Pastor White said the dedication of the new sanctuary was a milestone worth nothing.

Quote

If you could kick the person who causes most of your problems, you wouldn't be able to sit down for a month.

JOKE

A couple attended their first Lamaze class. Halfway through the class, the husband was given a bag of sand to strap around his waist to simulate being pregnant. The husband stood up and shrugged. "This doesn't feel so bad."

The instructor dropped a pen and asked the husband to pick it up.

"You want me to pick up the pen as if I were pregnant, the way my wife would do it?" the husband asked.

"Exactly," replied the instructor.

He looked at his wife and said, "Honey, pick up that pen for me."

52

BLOOPER

Please join us in celebrating Lint this season.

Quote

You are only young once; after that, you have to come up with some other excuse for your actions.

JOKE

Preparing for the most important presentation of his life, a sales rep decided to get help from a hypnotist. "I'll put a suggestion in your mind," said the hypnotist. "Just say '1-2-3,' and you'll give the presentation of your life. However, do not say '1-2-3-4,' because you'll freeze up and make a fool of yourself."

The sales rep was ecstatic. He tried it at home and impressed his family. He tried it at work and got a standing ovation. Then came the big day. In the boardroom, the CEO signaled the sales rep to start. The sales rep whispered confidently under his breath, "One-2-3."

Overhearing him, the CEO asked, "What did you say '1-2-3' for?"

53

Quote

It is generally agreed that some people are wise and some are otherwise.

JOKE

A visiting pastor was preaching in a church in Mississippi. When the host pastor announced that their prison quartet would be singing at the evening service, the visitor looked forward to hearing them even though he wasn't aware of any prison nearby.

The next night, when it was time for the special music, the visiting pastor was surprised to see 4 members of the congregation take the stage.

"This is our prison quartet," the host pastor said, with a smile. "Behind a few bars and always looking for the key."

54

BLOOPER

Mr. Peters said that his handmade chairs, normally priced $200, will be on sale next month for $199.99.

Quote

Everyone believes the Golden Rule—
give unto others the advice you can't use yourself.

JOKES

Official sign near door: Door Alarmed.
Hand-printed sign nearby: Window frightened.

Seen in a health food store: Shoplifters will be beaten over the head with an organic carrot.

On a repair shop door: We can repair anything. Please knock hard on the door—the bell doesn't work.

55

Have You Heard the One about . . .

A man kept bragging to his neighbor about how smart his bird dog was. Growing weary of the boasting, the neighbor finally said, "Let's see what that dog can really do."

Early the next morning, the trio tromped through a cotton field stopping at a small clump of bushes. The dog's owner sent the dog into the bushes. When the dog emerged, he patted his foot one time. "There's 1 bird in that bush," said the owner. He gave the command and the dog flushed out 1 bird.

Walking on, they came to a 2nd clump of bushes and repeated the exercise. This time the dog patted his foot twice. "There are 2 birds in the bush," said the owner. Sure enough, the dog flushed 2 birds.

The 2 men and the bird dog approached a corner full of bushes. Once again, the dog disappeared. After a minute, he ran out of the bushes and went berserk. He yanked cotton off the stalks with his teeth, and then he grabbed a stick and started shaking it vigorously.

"What is wrong with that crazy dog?" asked the neighbor.

"He's saying that there are more cotton-picking birds in that bush than you can shake a stick at."

56

BLOOPER

Our prayers go out to Dave Weigman, who shot himself in the leg while hunting mushrooms.

Quote

Be careful if you live in the lap of luxury because luxury might stand up.

JOKE

Before your next camping trip, remember the following:
   When using a public campground, a tuba placed on your picnic table will keep the campsites on either side vacant.

   Lint from your navel makes a handy fire starter. Warning: Remove lint from navel before applying the match.

   In an emergency, a drawstring from a parka hood can be used to strangle a snoring tent mate.

BLOOPER

Performing tonight are the Clause twins, Heather and Holly. Heather is 9 and Holly is 7.

Quote

Why is it that the fewer the facts, the stronger the opinion?

JOKE

A van filled with politicians was heading down a country road when, suddenly, the van careened off the road and crashed into a tree near a farmer's field. A farmer out plowing his field saw what happened. After investigating, he proceeded to bury all the politicians.

A few days later the local sheriff came out, saw what was left of the van, and asked the farmer where all the politicians had gone.

"I buried them."

"Were they *all* dead?"

"Well, some of them said they weren't," the farmer admitted, "but you know how them politicians lie."

58

BLOOPER

Cross Roads adult Sunday school class is offering free accounting tips from Scott Sloppy, CPA. Scott says that Sloppy Accounting honors biblical principles.

Quote

Nothing makes a child as smart as having grandparents.

JOKE

A husband and wife were at a party talking with some friends when the subject of marriage counseling came up.

"Oh, we'll never need that. My husband and I have a great relationship," the wife explained. "He was a communications major in college, and I majored in theater. He communicates very well, and I just act like I'm listening."

59

BLOOPER

Monday, March 5, is Ash Wednesday at All Souls Church in Dorchester.

Quote

Live your life so the preacher won't have to lie at your funeral.

JOKE

A minister was invited to dinner by one of his parishioners, a woman known for being a notoriously bad housekeeper.

When he sat down at the table, he noticed that the dishes were the dirtiest that he had ever seen in his life. "Have these dishes ever been washed?" he asked his hostess.

"They're as clean as soap and water could get them," she answered confidently.

The minister was apprehensive, but blessed the food anyway and started eating. Surprisingly, the food was really delicious and he complimented the hostess on her fine cooking. But when dinner was over, he almost lost it when the hostess took the dishes outside and yelled, "Here Soap! Here Water!"

60

Part 1
Real Good Writing Hints

* Verbs HAS to agree with their subjects.

* Prepositions are not words to end sentences with.

* And don't start a sentence with a conjunction.

* It is wrong to ever split an infinitive.

* Avoid clichés like the plague. (They're old hat.)

* Also, always avoid annoying alliteration.

* Be more or less specific.

* Parenthetical remarks (however relevant) are (usually) unnecessary.

* Also too, never, ever use repetitive redundancies.

* No sentence fragments.

* Contractions aren't necessary and shouldn't be used.

* Do not be redundant; do not use more words than necessary; it's highly superfluous.

* Don't use no double negatives.

* Eschew ampersands & abbreviations, etc.

* One-word sentences? Eliminate.

61

BLOOPER

Hazel Fisher claims her weight-loss system is permanent—as long as you don't gain the weight back.

Quote

The man who toots his own horn soon has everybody dodging him when he approaches.

JOKE

A man gets a telephone call from his doctor. The doctor says: "About your recent test: I have some good news and some bad news."

The man asks for the good news first.

"The good news is that you have 24 hours to live," says the doctor.

Incredulous, the man asks, "If that is the good news, then what is the bad news?"

"I couldn't reach you yesterday."

62

BLOOPER

The Olsens of Bridle Lane Lutheran are offering their home as a bed-and-breakfast for the summer. They have three guest rooms, a private bath, and color TV. Sorry, no breakfast.

Quote

If you really want to look tall, pick short friends.

JOKE

In an effort to test windshield strength, scientists at NASA have developed a bazooka-like gun to launch dead chickens toward airliners, military aircraft, and space shuttles traveling at maximum velocity. The chickens represent the average size of any number of birds commonly involved in dangerous flight collisions.

British engineers were eager to test the gun on the windshields of their new high-speed trains. When the gun was fired, the chicken smashed the "shatterproof" shield, crashed through the control console, snapped the engineer's headrest in two, and embedded itself in the wall of the cab.

Horrified Britons sent NASA the disastrous results, along with all the windshield specs.

NASA's response: "Thaw the chicken."

63

The minutes spent at the dinner table will not make you fat—the seconds will.

JOKE

Shooting the breeze down at the VA hospital, a trio of old-timers ran out of their own heroic tales so they started bragging about their ancestors. "When my great-grandfather was 13," one declared proudly, "he was a drummer boy at Shiloh."

"Mine," boasted another, "went down with Custer at the Battle of Little Big Horn."

"I'm the only soldier in my family," confessed the 3rd vet. "But if my great-grandfather were living today, he'd be the most famous man in the world."

"What'd he do?" his friends asked.

"Nothing. But he would be 165 years old."

64

BLOOPER

Anyone not claiming lost articles will be disposed of.

Quote

A person should give a lot of thought to sudden decisions.

JOKE

While making rounds, a doctor points out an X-ray to a group of medical students. "As you can see," she said, "the patient limps because his left fibula and tibia are radically arched."

Turning to the student next to her, the doctor asked, "What would you do in a case like this?"

"I suppose I'd limp too."

65

Part 1
Dictionary for Women

✳ Airhead: What a woman intentionally becomes when pulled over by a policeman.

✳ Argument: A discussion that occurs when you're right, but he just hasn't realized it yet.

✳ Barbecue: You bought the groceries, washed the lettuce, chopped the tomatoes, diced the onions, marinated the meat, and cleaned everything up, but he "made the dinner."

✳ Childbirth: You get to go through 36 hours of contractions; he gets to hold your hand and say, "Focus . . . breathe . . . push."

✳ Clothes dryer: An appliance designed to eat socks.

✳ Diet soda: A drink you buy at a convenience store to go with a half-pound bag of peanut M&Ms.

✳ Eternity: The last 2 minutes of a football game.

✳ Exercise: Doing multiple circuits of the mall, occasionally resting to make a purchase.

66

BLOOPER

Red tape at city hall holds up our new sanctuary.

Quote

A fanatic is a man who does what he thinks God would do if only God knew all the facts in the case.

JOKE

A computer programmer for a consulting group had designed some software for one of the company's largest accounts. He asked one of his coworkers for help in putting it into operation.

At first, he handled most of the work. Eventually, though, he asked his coworker to help out with the last phase of training. Sitting down with one woman, the coworker explained that he would be showing her how to make changes to the files. "I'm so glad you're the one who is teaching me, not him," the woman sighed in relief.

Surprised, the coworker commented that the programmer was far more experienced than he was.

"Yes," the woman said, "but I get nervous around really smart people."

BLOOPER

Stan Berts will teach a first-aid class this Wednesday evening at 7 p.m. Also included will be a demonstration of the Hemlock maneuver.

Quote

Bigamy is when 2 rites make a wrong.

JOKE

A man approached a beautiful woman in a huge supermarket and said, "I've gotten separated from my wife somewhere in this store. Can you talk to me for a couple of minutes?"

"Why?" she asks.

"Because every time I talk to a beautiful woman, my wife suddenly appears out of nowhere, and I'm tired of looking for her!"

68

BLOOPER

A note from newlyweds John and Cynthia Rusk: "Thank you all for coming to our wedding. It was beautiful that you brought our happiness to a conclusion."

Quote

A study of economics usually reveals that the best time to buy anything is last year.

JOKE

After church one Sunday, a young boy announced to his mother, "Mom, I've decided I'm going to be a minister when I grow up."

"How nice," the mother said. "What made you decide to become a minister?"

"Well," the boy replied, "since I'll have to go to church on Sunday anyway, I figure it will be more fun to stand up and yell than to sit still and listen."

BLOOPER

During the recent rains, the water was so high that the township had to evaporate portions of the city south of the tracks.

Quote

Show me a twin birth, and I will show you an infant replay.

JOKES

Bouncing out of her 1st day in church nursery school, a 3-year-old girl gleefully informed her mother: "We had juice and Billy Graham crackers!"

The church school's story and activity focused on Moses and the exodus from Egypt. When the children came upstairs, a 5-year-old girl excitedly greeted her mother: "Guess what? We made unleaded bread!"

70

Excuses for Missing Work

I can't come in to work today because I'll be stalking my previous boss, who fired me for not showing up for work.

I seem to have contracted some attention-deficit disorder, and hey, how about them Cubs, huh? So I won't be able to; yes, could I help you? No, no, I'll be sticking with Sprint, but thank you for calling.

I just found out that I was switched at birth. Legally, I shouldn't come to work because my employee records may now contain false information.

The EPA has determined that my house is completely surrounded by wetlands. I have to arrange for helicopter transportation.

I set half the clocks in my house ahead an hour and the other half back an hour Saturday and spent 18 hours in some kind of space-time continuum loop, reliving Sunday (right up until the explosion). I was able to exit the loop only by reversing the polarity of the power source for all of the clocks in the house. Accordingly, I will be in late or early.

BLOOPER

The celebration was a much-needed change at the church. We haven't heard laughing like that since Pastor Sears passed away.

Quote

If you want your landlord to paint your apartment, move out.

JOKE

While ferrying workers back and forth from the offshore oil rig, the helicopter lost power and went down. Fortunately, it landed safely in a lake. Struggling to get out, one man tore off his seat belt, inflated his life vest, and jerked open the exit door.

"Don't jump!" the pilot called out. "This thing floats!"

As the man leapt out the door of the helicopter, he yelled back, "Yeah, and it's supposed to fly too!"

BLOOPER

Jim Wilson, church chairman, urged the congregation to put principles aside and do what was right.

Quote

Neurotic means he is not as sensible as I am; *psychotic* means he's even worse than my brother-in-law.

JOKES

Actual call to the IRS: Hi, I'm a bookkeeper, and I need to know if ten $100 bills make $1,000 or only ten hundred dollars.
IRS: Both. It's the same amount.
Caller: So why do I get a different answer every time I move the decimal point?

Actual call to the IRS: Could you please send me some of those WD-40s?

73

Quote

They have perfected a new aspirin tablet—half aspirin and half glue. It's great for splitting headaches.

JOKE

A man learned shortly before quitting time that he had to attend a meeting. He tried unsuccessfully to locate his car-pool members to let them know that he would not be leaving with them.

He hastily scribbled a message to one fellow and left it on his desk: "I have a last-minute meeting. Leave without me."

At 7:00 p.m. the man came back to his desk and found this note: "Meet us at the coffee shop across the street. You drove!"

74

BLOOPER

For those in the congregation who need help with accounting and tax preparation, call John Cheater of Oxford Bible Church.

Quote

Don't ever take a fence down until you know the reason it was put up in the first place.

JOKE

It's their first day in heaven, and everyone is milling around. So God says, "I want the men to make 2 lines: one for husbands who dominated their wives; the other for husbands whose wives dominated them. As for the women, all of you follow St. Peter."

An hour later, God inspects the 2 lines. The line of men whose wives dominated them is 100 miles long. In the other line, there is only one man.

God said to the men in the endless line, "You should be ashamed. I created you in my image, but you let your wives dominate you. There is only one man who stood up for himself." Turning to the husband in the other line, God said, "Tell us, how did you manage to be the only person in this line?"

"I don't know," the man replied. "My wife told me to stand here."

75
Famous Last Words

Don't unplug it. This will just take a moment to fix.

We won't need reservations.

It's always sunny there this time of the year.

Don't worry; it's not loaded.

No problem. You can make it. That train isn't coming fast.

Gimmee a match. I think my gas tank is empty.

Just watch me dive from that bridge.

What happens if you touch these two wires tog—

What? Your mother is going to stay another month?

No, dude, this stuff is completely natural and safe.
That's why it's called "herbal," man.

76

BLOOPER

Dr. Wallace, speaking to the youth group last Wednesday, stated that boys cause as many teenage pregnancies as girls.

Quote

If you want to know what a man is truly like, put him in a position of authority.

JOKE

An artist asked the gallery owner if there had been any interest in his paintings that were on display.

"I have good news and bad news," the owner replied. "The good news is that a gentleman inquired about your work and wondered if the value of your paintings would appreciate after your death. When I told him they probably would, he bought all 15 of your paintings."

"That's wonderful," the artist exclaimed. "What's the bad news?"

"The guy was your doctor."

77

BLOOPER

Friday's "Meal and Message" will be cooked boneless man, with apricot sauce.

Quote

The best gift for a man who has everything
is a burglar alarm.

JOKE

Two men walked into a diner that looked as though it had seen better days. Before sitting down in the booth, the younger man brushed crumbs off the seat. Then he took a napkin and wiped some ketchup off the table.

The waitress came over and asked if they wanted menus. "No, thanks," said the older man. "I'll just have a cup of black coffee."

"I'll have black coffee, too," the younger man said. Then he added snippily, "And make sure the cup is clean."

The waitress shot him a nasty look before marching off into the kitchen.

Two minutes later, she was back.

"Two cups of black coffee," she announced curtly. "Which one of you wanted the clean cup?"

78

BLOOPER

Please join us for the marriage celebration of John Dusey and Carol Hinler—a sacrament that ignites a man and a woman.

Quote

If you can't win—make the fellow ahead of you break the record.

JOKE

One woman was bragging to her next-door neighbor about her son, a college student. "Why, our son is so brilliant, every time we get a letter from him we have to go to the dictionary."

"You're lucky," the neighbor said. "Every time we get a letter from ours, we have to go to the bank!"

BLOOPER

The $55 cost of the Prayer and Fasting Conference
at Thomasville Christian includes meals.

Quote

Two can live as cheaply as one—
if one of them doesn't eat.

JOKE

After a long night at the tavern, the man was in no shape
to drive, so he wisely left his car parked and walked
home. Seeing him stumbling down the sidewalk, a cop
pulled over and got out of the squad car.

"What are you doing out here at 2 a.m.?" asked the cop.

"I'm going to a lecture."

"Who is going to give a lecture at this hour?"

"My wife," said the man.

80

Alternative Meanings

* **Coffee:** A person who is coughed upon.

* **Flabbergasted:** Appalled over how much weight you have gained.

* **Abdicate:** To give up all hope of ever having a flat stomach.

* **Esplanade:** To attempt an explanation while drunk.

* **Negligent:** Describes a condition in which you absentmindedly answer the door in your nightie.

* **Lymph:** To walk with a lisp.

* **Gargoyle:** An olive-flavored mouthwash.

* **Flatulence:** The emergency vehicle that picks you up after you are run over by a steamroller.

* **Balderdash:** A rapidly receding hairline.

* **Rectitude:** The formal, dignified demeanor assumed by a proctologist immediately before he examines you.

* **Oyster:** A person who sprinkles his conversation with Yiddish expressions.

* **Frisbeetarianism:** The belief that, when you die, your soul goes up on the roof and gets stuck there.

* **Pokemon:** A Jamaican proctologist.

81

BLOOPER

Church newsletter classifieds: Daybed for sale.
Can also be used at night.

Quote

A fair-weather friend is one who is
always around when he needs you.

JOKES

Q: What do you get when you cross an elephant and
a skin doctor?
A: A pachydermatologist.

Q: What has 4 legs; is big, green, and fuzzy; and if it fell
out of a tree, it would kill you?
A: A pool table.

Q: What kind of coffee was served on the Titanic?
A: Sanka.

BLOOPER

As you can see from the attached drawing, our church addition will feature large, see-through windows.

Quote

Everything happens to everybody
sooner or later if there is time enough.

JOKE

A man woke up one morning to find that his wife had died in her sleep. He called 911.

"We'll send someone out right away," the dispatcher said. "Where do you live?"

"At the end of Eucalyptus Drive," the man replied.

"Can you spell that for me?"

There was a long pause. Finally the man said, "How 'bout if I drag her over to Oak Street and you pick her up there?"

83

Quote

Ambition may be all right, but it sure can get a fellow into
a lot of hard work.

JOKE

A traffic safety consultant often gave talks on accident
prevention. One night after he spoke to a PTA group, the
program chairperson thanked him profusely and gave him
a check for $50.

"Giving these presentations is a part of my job," the
consultant said. "Could I donate the money to one of your
causes?"

"That would be wonderful!" the chairperson said.
"I know just the program that needs it the most. We're
trying to raise money so we can afford better speakers."

84

BLOOPER

Notice soliciting prayers for families suffering loss: "Only a few of the deceased have been sent in. You can still bring yours with you to the meeting."

Quote

A baby boomer is someone who hires someone to cut the grass so he can play golf for exercise.

JOKE

A man died, and his family anxiously gathered together for the reading of his will.

"To my dear wife, I leave the house, 50 acres of land, and 10 million dollars. To my son, I leave my Lexus, Jaguar, Ferrari, and $500,000. To my daughter, I leave my yacht and $500,000. To my sister, I leave $250,000. And to my brother-in-law, who always insisted that health is better than wealth, I leave my sunlamp and barbells."

85

Things I Learned from Noah

* Plan ahead. It wasn't raining when Noah built the ark.

* Stay fit. When you're 600 years old, someone might ask you to do something *really* big.

* Build on high ground.

* For safety's sake, travel in pairs.

* Speed isn't always an advantage. The cheetahs were on board, but so were the snails.

* If you can't fight or flee—float!

* Take care of your animals as if they were the last ones on earth.

* Don't forget that we're all in the same boat.

* When the doo-doo gets really deep, don't sit there and complain—shovel!!!

* Stay below deck during the storm.

* Remember that the woodpeckers *inside* are often a bigger threat than the storm outside.

* No matter how bleak it looks, there's always a rain-bow on the other side.

BLOOPER

Pastor Mitchell has returned from Egypt where he took many photos of the pyramids—the ancient, huge, triangular stone cubes in the desert.

Quote

A joint checking account is never overdrawn by the wife.
It is simply underdeposited by her husband.

JOKE

A young man was sitting in class on the first day of law school when the professor asked him if he knew what the *Roe v. Wade* decision was.

After a lot of thought, the student said, "That was the decision George Washington made prior to crossing the Delaware."

BLOOPER

Wanted: Head liberian for the church library.
Must have some librarian experience.

Quote

It is difficult to save money when your neighbors keep
buying things you can't afford.

JOKES

A little boy was looking through his grandmother's old
Bible when something fell out. There on the floor was a
leaf that had been pressed between the pages. The boy
picked it up and examined it closely before shouting,
"Look, Mommy! I found Adam's suit!"

Two atoms were walking down the street when one atom
says to the other, "I've lost an electron!"
   "Are you sure?" asked the other atom.
   "I'm positive."

88

BLOOPER

We have had a report on former student minister Roy Tempers, who has been in a car accident and suffered at least 2 broken legs.

Quote

There are 3 chief causes of divorce in America today—men, women, and marriage.

JOKE

A ventriloquist is onstage, and midway through his performance throws in a series of blonde jokes. Suddenly, a blonde stands on her chair and shouts, "I've heard just about enough of your blonde jokes! It's guys like you who keep women like me from being respected."

Flustered, the ventriloquist begins to apologize.

To which the blonde interjects, "You stay out of this, mister. I'm talking to the little guy!"

BLOOPER

Academy lunch menu: Wednesday—soup of the day
is soup du jour.

Quote

He knows so little and knows it so fluently.

JOKE

At a marriage seminar on communication, the presenter
declared: "It is essential that husbands and wives know
the things that are important to each other. For instance,
gentlemen, can you name your wife's favorite flower?"

One attendee leaned over, touched his wife's arm
gently, and whispered, "Pillsbury All-Purpose, isn't it?"

Part 2

Real Good Writing Hints

* Analogies in writing are like feathers on a snake.

* The passive voice is to be ignored.

* Eliminate commas, that are, not necessary. Parenthetical words however should be enclosed in commas.

* Never use a big word when a diminutive one would suffice.

* Kill all exclamation points!!!

* Use words correctly, irregardless of how others use them.

* Use the apostrophe in it's proper place and omit it when its not needed.

* Eliminate quotations. As Ralph Waldo Emerson said, "I hate quotations. Tell me what you know."

* If you've heard it once, you've heard it a thousand times: Resist hyperbole; not one writer in a million can use it correctly.

* Puns are for children, not groan readers.

* Who needs rhetorical questions?

BLOOPER

Libby McDowell is seeking a part-time sitter for her well-behaved 5-year-old; 1-year-old refrigerator and 2-year-old stove. Great condition.

Quote

A minor operation is one that is performed on someone else.

JOKE

A woman, obviously greatly agitated, rushed to see her doctor.

"Doctor, when I woke up this morning and looked in the mirror, my hair was all frazzled, my skin was pasty, and my eyes were bloodshot and bugging out. I looked like a corpse! What's wrong with me?"

"Well, I can tell you one thing," the doctor calmly replied. "There's nothing wrong with your eyesight."

92

BLOOPER

Stevensville Bible Academy students watched as city workers cut down several trees to mark the Arbor Day celebration.

Quote

You live only once—but if you work it right, once is enough.

JOKE

Before entering a little country store, a stranger noticed a sign on the door: Danger! Beware of Dog! Inside, he saw an old hound dog asleep on the floor beside the cash register.

"Is that the dog folks are supposed to beware of?" he asked the storekeeper.

"Yep, that's him," he replied.

"He sure doesn't look that dangerous to me. Why the sign?"

"Because," the storekeeper replied, "before I posted that sign, people kept tripping over him."

BLOOPER

The Sunday school Easter-egg hunt will be from 10:00 to 10:03. Don't be late or your child may miss the excitement.

Quote

I solved the parking problem.
I bought a parked car.

JOKE

A man and his wife went to the mall together. "Take your time, honey," the husband said. "While you're shopping, I'll go browse in the hardware store."

An hour later, the wife spotted her husband at the hardware checkout counter with 2 cartloads of tools and supplies.

"Are you buying all this?" his wife asked incredulously.

"Well, yes," he said. Then gesturing toward the rest of the store, he added, "But look at all the stuff I'm leaving behind!"

94

BLOOPER

Reverend Tim Wilson, his wife, and his mother-in-law have visited all 61 states and many foreign countries.

Quote

When a billing clerk goes psycho,
he hears strange invoices.

JOKE

A young boy called the pastor of a small local church, asking him to come and pray for his mother, who was ill with the flu. The pastor knew the family and was aware they had been attending a much bigger church down the road. So the pastor asked, "Shouldn't you be asking the pastor of your own church to come and pray with your mom?"

"Yeah," the boy replied, "except we didn't want to take the chance that he might catch whatever she has."

95

Part 1
Aphorisms for Our Time

* Deja Moo: The feeling that you've heard this bull before.

* Clothes make the man. Naked people have little or no influence on society.

* If at first you don't succeed, skydiving is not for you.

* Money can't buy happiness. But it sure makes misery easier to live with.

* Vital papers will demonstrate their vitality by moving from where you left them to where you can't find them.

* Always remember to pillage *before* you burn.

* The trouble with doing something right the first time is that nobody appreciates how difficult it was.

* Ray's Law: You can't fall off the floor.

* Paranoids are people too; they have their own problems. It's easy to criticize, but if everybody hated you, you'd be paranoid too.

* Eagles may soar, but weasels aren't sucked into jet engines.

96

BLOOPER

The elders have decided to meet this next Wednesday to discuss when they should meet next.

Quote

It is always good to be careful when you give advice because someone actually might take it.

JOKE

After the school pictures were completed, the teacher was trying to persuade each student to buy a group picture. "Just think how nice it will be to look at it when you are all grown up and say, 'There's Jennifer; she's a lawyer,' or 'That's Michael; he's a doctor.'"

A small voice at the back of the room rang out, "And there's the teacher; she's dead."

BLOOPER

St. Francis High School plans to fight student boredom with longer classes.

Quote

Speak when you're angry, and you'll make the best speech you will ever regret.

JOKE

A man and his wife were having some problems at home, culminating in the silent treatment. This continued through the weekend. When the husband tried to set the alarm clock for the next morning, it didn't work. Since his wife always got up first, he needed her to wake him at 5:00 a.m. for a morning business flight. Not wanting to be the first to break the silence, he wrote on a piece of paper, "Please wake me at 5:00 a.m."

The next morning the man woke up at 7:00 a.m. Furious, he was about to yell at his wife when he noticed a piece of paper by the bed. The paper said, "It's 5:00 a.m. Wake up!"

98

BLOOPER

Bob Gellings will recount his dramatic rescue after being trapped on an escalator for more than 12 hours.

Quote

When I go to a fancy restaurant,
I always ask for a table near a waiter.

JOKE

Returning from a trip to visit her grandmother, a woman was pulled over by a state trooper for speeding. When the trooper gave her a verbal warning rather than writing a ticket, the grateful driver gave him a small bag of her grandmother's homemade chocolate chip cookies to thank him.

Ten miles down the road, another trooper stopped the same car. "But officer, I wasn't speeding, was I?" the woman asked.

"No," the trooper said with a smile. "But I heard you were passing out great chocolate chip cookies."

BLOOPER

The survey results are in. Our congregation is made up of 90 percent whites, 5 percent African-Americans, 5 percent Hispanics, and 5 percent Asian and others.

Quote

Yawning is usually the inadvertent act of opening your mouth when you wish the other person would shut theirs.

JOKE

The first day on the job, a new CEO decided to get rid of all the slackers in the company. Touring the facilities, the CEO noticed a guy leaning against a wall. The CEO walked up and asked, "How much money do you make a week?"

The young fellow shrugged and said, "I make $400 a week. Why?"

The CEO handed the guy $400 in cash and said, "Here's a week's pay, now *get out* and don't come back!"

Smiling, the guy took the cash and left.

The CEO asked the entourage with him, "Do any of you know what that slacker did here?"

"Yeah. He was a pizza delivery guy from Domino's."

100

Part 2

Manly Men Never Say . . .

* I'll take Shakespeare for 1,000, Alex;

* Honey, I think we should sell the pickup and buy a family sedan;

* We don't keep firearms in this house;

* I need the sideburns trimmer;

* You can't feed that to the dog;

* I thought Graceland was tacky;

* No kids in the back of the pickup—it's just not safe;

* Wrestling's fake;

* Honey, please mail that donation to Greenpeace;

* We're vegetarians;

* I don't have a favorite college team;

* Duct tape won't fix that.

BLOOPER

The church is sorry about the construction and any incontinence it has caused.

Quote

A person with a green thumb could be a great gardener or a lousy painter.

JOKE

In a comparative religions course, the students were listening to a lecture on psychic phenomena. The instructor mentioned a woman who contacted a police department working on a missing person case.

"She gave eerily detailed instructions on where to find the body," the instructor said. "In fact, the detectives did find the body just as she had described. Now, what would you call that kind of person?"

A sheriff taking the course immediately replied, "A suspect."

102

BLOOPER

Members of our youth group will provide housecleaning services at your house if necessary. Contact the church office for details.

Quote

When the majority agrees on an idiotic idea—
it is still an idiotic idea.

JOKE

The good-humored boss was compelled to call his delinquent employee into his office.

"It has not escaped my attention," the boss pointed out, "that every time there's a home game at the stadium you have to take your aunt to the doctor."

"You know you're right, sir," exclaimed the sports fan. "You don't suppose she's faking it, do you?"

BLOOPER

Church newsletter classifieds: For sale—playpen, mesh sides, hardly used. Perfect for grandma.

Quote

When life trips you up, be sure to pick something up on your way back up.

JOKES

Taking advantage of a balmy spring day, 4 ministers decided to get together for a friendly game of golf. After several really horrible holes and lots of terribly bad shots, their caddy asked, "You guys wouldn't be ministers by any chance?"

"Actually, yes, we are," a member of the group replied. "Why?"

"Because," said the caddy, "I've never seen such bad golf and heard such clean language!"

104

BLOOPER

We need volunteers for our auto repair ministry. If you know nothing about cars, you are encouraged to join.

Quote

Advertising helps raise the standard of living by raising the standard of longing.

JOKE

Two longtime bachelors were sitting and talking. Their conversation went from sports to cooking.

"I got a cookbook once," said the first, "but I could never do anything with it."

"Too many fancy recipes in it?" asked the second.

"You said it. Every recipe began the same way: 'Take a clean dish and . . .' "

105
Bumper Sticker Wisdom

Two wrongs don't make a right, but two Wrights made an airplane.

It's not the pace of life that concerns me; it's the sudden stop at the end.

The problem with the gene pool is that there is no lifeguard.

Living on Earth is expensive, but it does include a free trip around the sun every year.

The only time the world beats a path to your door is if you're in the bathroom.

If God wanted me to touch my toes, he would have put them on my knees.

Never knock on Death's door. Ring the doorbell and run. He hates that.

Lead me not into temptation. I can find the way myself.

106

BLOOPER

Fireman John O'Hare said that fire was the cause of the blaze that damaged our church kitchen.

Quote

How many pessimists wind up wanting the things they fear—just in order to prove that they are right?

JOKE

An exasperated mother, whose son was always getting into trouble, finally asked him, "How do you expect to get into heaven?"

The boy thought for a minute, then said, "Well, I'll just run in and out and in and out and keep slamming the door until St. Peter says, 'For heaven's sake, Jimmy, come in or stay out!' "

BLOOPER

Join us at the jobs seminar next Tuesday. Learn how to find a job and stop looking for work.

Quote

Instead of crying over spilled milk,
milk another cow.

JOKE

A husband and wife got into a petty argument. Neither of them would admit the possibility that the other might be in error.

To her credit, the wife finally said, "Look. I'll admit I'm wrong if you admit I was right."

"Fine," her husband said.

She took a deep breath, looked her husband in the eye and said, "I'm wrong."

With a big grin, her husband replied, "You're right."

108

Quote

When arguing with a stupid person,
make sure he isn't doing the same thing.

JOKE

A blonde was playing Trivial Pursuit. When her turn came around, she rolled the dice and landed on "Science and Nature."

The question was: "If you are in a vacuum and someone calls your name, can you hear it?"

With a thoughtful look she asked, "Is it on or off?"

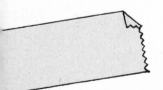

BLOOPER

After today's service, the dress committee would like to see all the women who haven't finished their dresses in the front.

Quote

Early to bed and early to rise is a sure sign that you're fed up with television.

JOKE

A Texan, anticipating an upcoming wedding, told his future son-in-law that he wanted his daughter to have her great grandmother's diamond ring. But first he wanted to have it appraised. The Texan contacted a gemologist friend who agreed to determine the ring's value. Instead of a fee, she suggested lunch at one of Houston's finer restaurants as payment.

A few days later, as the Texan and the gem expert sat sipping a glass of Chablis, he showed her the ring. She took out her jeweler's loupe, examined the diamond carefully, and handed it back.

"Wow," said a diner watching from the next table. "These Texas women are tough!"

110

Inspirational Cubicle Posters

Rome did not create a great empire by having meetings. They did it by killing all those who opposed them.

If you can stay calm while all around you is chaos, you probably haven't completely understood the seriousness of the situation.

Artificial Intelligence is no match for Natural Stupidity.

A person who smiles in the face of adversity probably has a scapegoat.

If at first you don't succeed, try management.

Never put off until tomorrow what you can avoid altogether.

Teamwork means never having to take all the blame yourself.

111

BLOOPER

Reverend Hanks said that the official policy of the church supports capital punishment, but only for the guilty.

Quote

Ask your child what he wants for dinner
only if he's buying.

JOKE

Defendant: Your honor, I want you to appoint me another lawyer.
Judge: And why is that?
Defendant: Because the public defender isn't interested in my case.
Judge (to public defender): Do you have any comments on the defendant's motion?
Public defender: I'm sorry, your honor. I wasn't listening.

112

BLOOPER

For those still alive at the end of the sermon, please stand and join us in a closing song.

Quote

The art of being wise is in knowing what to overlook.

JOKE

A teenage girl nervously took the wheel for her first driving lesson. As she was pulling out of the parking lot, the instructor said, "Turn left here, and don't forget to let the people behind you know what you're doing."

The young girl immediately turned to the students sitting in the backseat and announced, "I'm going left."

113

Quote

There are some people who are so addicted to exaggeration they can't tell the truth without lying.

JOKE

An elderly couple is lying in bed one morning, having just awakened from a good night's sleep.

Reaching for his wife's hand, the husband is startled when she responds, "Don't touch me."

"Why not?"

"Because I'm dead."

"What do you mean? We're talking to one another."

"No, I'm definitely dead," the wife insists.

"You're not dead. What in the world makes you think you're dead?"

"Because nothing hurts!"

114

BLOOPER

During this year's Vacation Bible School, the Redeemed Evangelical Center will host a daily buffet that will be served daily.

Quote

Good judgment comes from experience—and experience, well, that comes from poor judgment.

JOKE

A father found his 4-year-old daughter outside brushing their dog's teeth, using his toothbrush.

"What are you doing with my toothbrush?" the father said in alarm.

"I'm cleaning Rocket's teeth," the daughter answered sweetly. "But don't worry, Dad. I'll rinse it out when I'm done just like I always do."

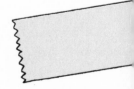

Part 2

Funny Definitions

Consist: A growth on an inmate.

Content: A fabric shelter for inmates.

Convent: How inmates get air conditioning.

Counterfeiters: Workers who put together kitchen working surfaces.

Crestfallen: Dropped toothpaste.

Cross-eyed teacher: A teacher who loses control over his or her pupils.

Decrease: De fold in de pants.

Demote: What de king put around de castle.

Despise: De persons who work for de CIA.

Detention: What causes de stress.

Dictator: Another name for Richard Spud.

Dilate: When a person lives longer.

Dreadlocks: The fear of opening the dead bolt.

116

Quote

Old age is when you find yourself using
one bend-over to pick up 2 things.

JOKE

Two women, girlfriends since grade school, had both
been married to their respective husbands for a long time.
One day, the 1st girlfriend is commiserating with her
longtime friend on the phone.

"I don't think my husband finds me attractive anymore,"
she sobbed. "As I get older, he doesn't bother to look
at me!"

"I'm sorry," her friend said. "As I get older, my husband
says I get more beautiful every day."

"Yes, but your husband's an antique dealer!"

117

BLOOPER

Margaret Sater and Jeffery Wilson will be joined in holy acrimony this Saturday at 3 p.m. in the north sanctuary. All are invited to attend.

Quote

A budget is a formula for determining that you need a raise.

JOKE

Two elderly women were out driving. Cruising along, they came to an intersection. The stoplight was red, but the driver kept going. Alarmed, the passenger thought, *I must be losing it. I could have sworn we just went through a red light.*

They came to another red light. Again, they drove right through. Again, the passenger questioned her sanity, but kept quiet. Still, she was getting nervous.

At the 3rd intersection, sure enough, it happened again. The passenger couldn't let it go this time. She turned to her friend and said, "Mildred, did you know that we just ran 3 red lights in a row? You could have killed us both!"

Mildred said, "Oh, my! Am I driving?"

118

Quote

Criticism wouldn't be so hard to take
if it weren't so often right.

JOKE

A young lady came home from a date, looking sad. "Anthony proposed to me an hour ago," she told her mother.

"Then why are you so sad?"

"Because he also told me he is an atheist. Mom, he doesn't even believe in hell."

"Marry him anyway," her mother replied. "Between the two of us, we'll show him how wrong he is."

BLOOPER

At the recent meeting of the women's guild, Dr. Larsen suggested that people should check with their doctors before getting sick.

Quote

At 50, everyone has the face he deserves.

JOKE

While discussing the challenges that DMV examiners face, a former motor vehicle bureau director recounted the story about one woman's final driving test.

On her first attempt at parallel parking, the examiner asked calmly, "Could you get a little closer?"

Without hesitating, she slid next to him.

120

Household Handyman's Guide

* If you can't find a screwdriver, use a knife. If you break off the tip, it's an improved screwdriver.

* Try to work alone. An audience is rarely any help.

* Work in the kitchen whenever you can. There are many fine tools there, it's warm and dry, and you are close to the refrigerator.

* If it's electronic, get a new one. Or consult a 12-year-old.

* Keep it simple: Get a new battery; replace the bulb or fuse; see if the tank is empty; try turning the switch "on"; or just paint over it.

* Always take credit for miracles. If you dropped the alarm clock while taking it apart and it suddenly starts working, you have healed it.

* Regardless of what people say, kicking, pounding, or throwing sometimes *will* help.

* Above all, if what you've done is stupid but it works, then it isn't stupid.

BLOOPER

Replacement for narthex window blocked by board.

Quote

He was a self-made man who owed his
lack of success to no one.

JOKE

A woman approached the minister after a church service,
quite embarrassed. "I hope you didn't take it personally,
Reverend, when my husband walked out during your
sermon."

   "I did find it a bit disconcerting," the preacher replied.

   "It's not a reflection on you," insisted the churchgoer.
"Ralph has been walking in his sleep ever since he was
a child."

122

BLOOPER

The prelude will contain sections of the "Unfinished Symphony" by Sherbet.

Quote

Reading what people write on desks, in public restrooms, and on trees can teach you a lot.

JOKE

As my 5-year-old son and I were headed to McDonald's one day, we saw a car accident up ahead. Usually when we see something terrible like that, we say a quick prayer for anyone who might be hurt. So I said to my son, "We should pray."

From the backseat I heard his earnest request: "Please, God, don't let those cars be blocking the entrance to McDonald's."

BLOOPER

The church office will be closed until opening. It will remain closed after being opened. Open tomorrow.

Quote

My lawyer made me tell the truth—
he said he would do anything to win his case.

JOKE

Three buddies die in a car crash and go to an orientation in heaven.

They are all asked, "When you are in your casket and friends and family are mourning you, what would you like to hear them say about you?"

The 1st guy says, "I would like to hear them say that I was a great doctor and a wonderful family man."

The 2nd guy says, "I would like to hear them say that I was a good husband and a schoolteacher who made a huge difference in the lives of many children."

The last guy replies, "I would like to hear them say, 'Look—he's moving!'"

124

BLOOPER

Pastor Wilkey said it was a once-in-a-lifetime experience, and "those only happen every so often."

Quote

All marriages are happy. It's the living together afterward that causes all the trouble.

JOKE

Teacher: How old were you on your last birthday?
Student: Seven.
Teacher: How old will you be on your next birthday?
Student: Nine.
Teacher: That's impossible.
Student: No, it isn't, teacher. I'm 8 today.

Part 2

Travel Language

Tour Guide Says:	*Translation:*
Nominal fee	Outrageous charge
Standard	Substandard
Deluxe	Standard
Superior	One free shower cap
All the amenities	Two free shower caps
Plush	Top and bottom sheets
Gentle breezes	Occasional gale-force winds
Light and airy	No air conditioning
Picturesque	Noisy theme park next door

126

BLOOPER

Our speaker at the men's fraternity lunch this Saturday will be William Stough, who works for a large import-outport bank.

Quote

When you have told someone that you plan to leave them your fortune, the only decent thing to do is to die quickly.

JOKE

Adam was walking around the Garden of Eden feeling lonely, so God asked, "What is wrong with you?"

Adam said he didn't have anyone to talk to.

God said he would give him a woman for a companion. She would be a good cook. She would always agree with Adam's decisions. She would bear his children. She would not nag and would always admit she was wrong after a disagreement. She would never have a headache and would freely give love and compassion.

"What would a woman like this cost me?" Adam asked.

God said, "An arm and a leg."

Adam said, "What can I get for a rib?"

BLOOPER

Youth Pastor Haney started the Youth Fest by announcing that everyone was there to have a good time whether they liked it or not.

Quote

There are two kinds of secrets: one is not worth keeping, and the other is too good to keep.

JOKE

Back in my day we didn't have MTV or inline skates. The latest rock 'n' roll hits were on 45s, and roller skates had metal wheels—you used a skate key to adjust the length of the frame to your foot. The 45s always skipped, so to get them to play right, you'd weigh the needle down with something heavy, like quarters, which we never had because our allowances were too small. So we'd use our skate keys instead and end up forgetting they were taped to the record player arm. That meant we couldn't adjust our skates, which didn't really matter because, when you hit a pebble, those crummy metal wheels would kill you anyway.

128

> ## BLOOPER
> Our Easter service is always very popular. We suggest you get here early so you can get a seat in the back.

Quote

A speech is like a wheel—
the longer the spoke, the greater the tire.

JOKE

A fellow walked into a doctor's office, and when the receptionist asked him what he had he replied, "Shingles."

She took down his name, address, insurance information, and told him to have a seat. Ten minutes later a nurse came and asked him what he had.

"Shingles."

She took him in the back and did a complete workup. Twenty minutes later the doctor came in. "What are you here for?"

"Shingles."

"Where?" the doctor asked.

"In the truck. Where do you want them?"

BLOOPER

The choir and actors will meet Wednesday evening before the cantata for a stress rehearsal.

Quote

I have never been hurt by anything I didn't say.

JOKE

A retired minister made it a practice to visit the parish school one day each week. The 4th graders were studying the states, so when he dropped in on the class, he asked them how many states they could name. They could only come up with about 40 states.

The minister told them that in his day students knew the names of all the states.

To which one little boy replied, "Yes, but in those days there were only 13."

130
Bumper Sticker Wisdom

The mind is like a parachute; it works much better when it's open.

Never take life seriously. Nobody gets out alive anyway.

There are two kinds of pedestrians—the quick and the dead.

An unbreakable toy is useful for breaking other toys.

A closed mouth gathers no feet.

Good health is merely the slowest possible rate at which one can die.

It's not hard to meet expenses—they're everywhere.

The only difference between a rut and a grave is the depth.

BLOOPER

The sunrise Easter service was a great success—more than a dozen different abominations gathered at North Side Park.

Quote

Experience teaches best
because it gives you individual instruction.

JOKE

A Sunday school teacher was telling a group of 4-year-olds about Jesus, Joseph, and Mary. After the lesson the kids were asked to draw a picture depicting their favorite part of the story. The teacher received pictures of the baby Jesus in the manger surrounded by animals, pictures of the three wise men, and the like.

One drawing puzzled her. It was a picture of an airplane with 4 people in it. She called the artist up to explain his picture. He pointed out Mary, Joseph, and the baby Jesus, and said this was their "flight" to Egypt. The teacher then asked about the other man in the plane.

"Oh, that's Pontius, the pilot."

BLOOPER

Pat Hoffman accused the board chairman
of being impartial.

Quote

To exercise is human, not to is divine.

JOKE

"I am happy to see you," the little boy said to his
grandmother on his dad's side. "Now maybe my mom
will do the trick she's been promising us."

The grandmother was curious. "What trick is that?"

"I heard her tell Dad that she would climb the walls if
you came to visit," the boy answered innocently.

133

Quote

A poor man can be happy, but a happy man isn't poor.

JOKE

A woman who had procrastinated cleaning and organizing her house for a long time was planning to entertain a household of guests. The afternoon of the party, she phoned a friend, sounding glum.

"I went to the bookstore and bought a book on how to get organized," she explained. "I was all fired up and decided to clean out all the shelves in the living room. There I found the exact same book, because I had bought it a couple of years ago!"

134

BLOOPER

The evangelical crusade featuring Elroy Barton will be held Saturday and Sunday, April 31st and 32nd.

Quote

Some people are easily entertained.
All you have to do is sit down and listen to them.

JOKE

A young couple drove several miles down a country road, not saying a word. An earlier discussion had led to an argument, and neither wanted to concede their position.

As they passed a barnyard of mules and pigs, the husband sarcastically quipped, "Relatives of yours?"

"Yes," his wife replied. "I married into the family."

135

Inspirational Cubicle Posters

When the going gets tough, the tough take a coffee break.

Hang in there. Retirement is only 40 years away.

We waste time, so you don't have to.

Never underestimate the power of very crabby people in large groups.

Go the extra mile. It makes your boss look like an incompetent slacker.

A snooze button is a poor substitute for no alarm clock at all.

Indecision is the key to *flexibility*.

Aim low. Reach your goals. Avoid disappointment.

136

BLOOPER

Rusty Baines, our building superintendent, warns everyone that there may be water on the sidewalks when it rains. But this is only a temporary condition.

Quote

Only 2 things are needed to keep a wife happy. One is to let her think she is getting her own way, and the other is to let her have it.

JOKE

A pedestrian at an intersection steps off the curb to cross the street when a car comes careening around the corner and heads straight for him. The man speeds up, but the car changes lanes and is still coming at him.

The guy turns around to go back, but once again the car changes lanes. The car is so close that the man freezes in the middle of the road.

Coming within a foot of hitting the terrified man, the car swerves at the last possible second and screeches to a halt.

The driver rolls down the window. It's a squirrel. The squirrel says to the man, "See, it's not as easy as it looks, is it?"

137

BLOOPER

Due to the lack of sign-ups, the voluntary cleanup day at St. Mark's Church is now mandatory.

Quote

If you have to borrow money, borrow from a pessimist because that person won't expect to get paid back.

JOKE

There was once an aspiring veterinarian who put himself through school working nights as a taxidermist.

Upon graduation, he decided he could combine his two vocations to better serve the needs of his patients and their owners, while doubling his practice and his income.

The sign on his clinic door reads, "Dr. Jones, Veterinary Medicine and Taxidermy—Either way, you get your pet back!"

138

BLOOPER

Edna Mae Taylor, now 22 months pregnant, will be resigning as choir director next month. Best wishes on your new endeavor, Edna!

Quote

A radical is anyone whose opinions differ radically from mine.

JOKE

A blonde was terribly overweight, so her doctor put her on a diet. "I want you to eat regularly for 2 days, then skip a day. Repeat this procedure for 2 weeks. The next time I see you, you'll be at least 5 pounds lighter."

When the blonde returned two weeks later, the doctor was shocked when she got on the scale. She had lost nearly 20 pounds.

"Why, that's amazing!" the doctor said. "Did you follow my instructions?"

The blonde nodded, then added, "I'll tell you, though, I thought I was going to drop dead every 3rd day."

"From hunger?" asked the doctor.

"No, from skipping."

BLOOPER

Our missionary to the inner city, Pat Hingle, claimed that his neighborhood is safe—except for the murders.

Quote

Too many after-dinner speakers are merely after dinner.

JOKE

A man had 3 daughters and was certain that when they became old enough to date, he'd disapprove of every young man who took them out.

Yet when the time came, the father was pleasantly surprised. Each boy that each of his daughters brought home was delightful and well-mannered.

The father mentioned to one of his daughters that he liked all the young men she and her sisters had brought home.

"You know, of course, Dad, we don't show you everybody," she truthfully replied.

Part 1

Funny Instructions

For a hair dryer: Do not use while sleeping.

On a bag of Fritos: You could be a winner! No purchase necessary. Details inside.

On a bath bar: Use like regular soap.

On a frozen-dinner box: Serving suggestion—defrost.

On a hotel-provided shower-cap box: Fits one head.

On a package of tiramisu (printed on the bottom of the box): Do not turn upside down.

On English bread pudding: Product will be hot after heating.

In the instruction booklet for an iron: Do not iron clothes on body.

141

BLOOPER

Associate Pastor Bob Fiddler thanks everyone for the cards and calls concerning his broken arm. Working on his house, a strong wind blew Fiddler off the roof.

Quote

Worry is interest paid on trouble before it falls due.

JOKE

A pharmacist arrives at the drugstore and finds a nervous-looking fellow bracing himself against the wall. "What's with that guy over there by the wall?" the pharmacist asks the checkout clerk.

"Oh. He came in this morning to get something for his cough. I couldn't find the cough syrup, so I gave him a bottle of laxative to drink."

"What!" the pharmacist exclaims. "You can't treat a cough with a bottle of laxative!"

"Of course you can! Look at him. He's terrified to cough!"

142

BLOOPER

The Wilson Brothers Quartet features all 5 of the Wilson brothers.

Quote

Half the world is ready to tell the other half how to live.

JOKE

In the cafeteria of a parochial school, the children were lined up for lunch. At the beginning of the line was a large pile of apples. A nun had placed a note in front of the apples: "Take only one. God is watching."

Farther down the cafeteria line was a large pile of chocolate chip cookies. One of the boys wrote a note and placed it in front of the cookies: "Take all you want. God is watching the apples."

BLOOPER

The pastor warned the youth group about the movie
Harry Potter and the Chamber of Commerce.

Quote

Comfortable chairs are worn out from hard use.
Uncomfortable ones become antiques.

JOKE

Four old men were out golfing.

"These hills are getting steeper as the years go by,"
one complained.

"These fairways seem to be getting longer, too," said
another.

"The sand traps seem to be bigger than I remember
them," said the 3rd senior.

Hearing enough complaints from his senior buddies,
the oldest and the wisest of the foursome piped up: "Just
be thankful we're still on the right side of the grass!"

144

BLOOPER

The color guard at the Memorial Day prayer observance will consist of uninformed soldiers carrying the flag.

Quote

The advantage of having more than one child is that one may turn out well.

JOKE

A nursery school teacher was driving a van full of kids home one day when a fire truck zoomed past. Excited to see a dalmatian sitting in the front seat, the children began discussing what the dog's job was.

"They use him to keep the crowds back," said one youngster.

"No," said another, "he's just for good luck."

A 3rd child sealed the argument. "No, they use the dog to find the fire hydrants."

145

Part 2
Funny Instructions

On a bottle of sleeping pills: Warning—may cause drowsiness.

On a Korean kitchen knife: Warning—keep out of children.

On a string of Chinese-made Christmas lights: For indoor or outdoor use only.

On a Japanese food processor: Not to be used for the other use.

On a jar of peanuts: Warning—contains nuts.

On an airline package of nuts: Instructions—open package, eat nuts.

On a Swedish chainsaw: Do not attempt to stop chain with your hands.

On a package of raisins: Why not try tossing over your favorite breakfast cereal?

146

BLOOPER

In a special tribute to all the men who have led the nation, Pastor Hosfield reminded the congregation that he was taking Monday off.

Quote

Enough is usually a little more than we possess.

JOKE

A police car pulls in the driveway of a house. From out of the car, an elderly gentleman and policeman emerge, go to the front door, and ring the doorbell. An elderly woman answers the door and is startled to see her husband standing there with the officer. "We found him in the park," the polite policeman explains. "He said he was lost and couldn't find his way home."

"You've been going to that park for more than 40 years!" the man's wife said. "How could you get lost?"

Leaning over, the husband whispered, "I wasn't lost. I was just too tired to walk home."

BLOOPER

St. Matthew's All-Church Sunday night dinner will be served on Tuesdays this month.

Quote

Even when facts are ignored, they do not cease to exist.

JOKES

Teacher: Max, use *defeat, defense,* and *detail* in a sentence.
Max: De rabbit cut across de field, and defeat went over defense before detail.

Teacher: If I had 7 oranges in one hand and 8 oranges in the other, what would I have?
Student in the back: Big hands!

148

BLOOPER

Dr. Regswell told the group at the seminar that male infertility is a major problem and can be passed on to children.

Quote

No matter how long you nurse a grudge,
it won't get any better.

JOKE

A Western journalist in Jerusalem had an apartment overlooking the Wailing Wall. Every day she saw an old Jewish man fervently praying.

One day the journalist introduced herself to the old man. "How long have you been coming to the wall?" she asked. "What are you praying for?"

"I have come every day for 25 years. In the morning I pray for world peace and the brotherhood of man. I go home, have tea, and come back to pray for the eradication of illness and disease from the earth."

The journalist was amazed. "How does it make you feel to come here every day for 25 years and pray for these things?"

"Like I'm talking to a wall."

149

BLOOPER

The Ridge Road Presbyterian Church has gone to court with the Alwine School District, seeking to block the district's some-sex benefits.

Quote

Strategy is hiring a babysitter on a diet.

JOKES

In my day, we didn't have calculators. We had to do addition on our fingers. To subtract, we amputated them.

In my day, we didn't have water. We had to smash together our own hydrogen and oxygen atoms.

In my day, we didn't have virtual reality. If a barbarian was chasing you with an ax, you just had to hope you could outrun him.

150

Part 2
Aphorisms for Our Time

Experience is something you don't get until just after you need it.

To steal ideas from one person is plagiarism; to steal from many is research.

To succeed in politics, it is often necessary to rise above your principles.

The sooner you fall behind, the more time you'll have to catch up.

A clear conscience is usually the sign of a bad memory.

If you must choose between two evils, pick the one you've never tried before.

Change is inevitable . . . except from vending machines.

Hard work pays off in the future. Laziness pays off now.

If at first you don't succeed, destroy all evidence that you tried.

A conclusion is the place where you got tired of thinking.

BLOOPER

Bud Knauf recounted his battle back from poverty. "I was working in a nursing home. Emptying bedpans allowed me to put food on the table for my family."

Quote

Life may begin at 40, but you miss a lot
if you wait until then.

JOKE

Sherlock Holmes and Dr. Watson were on a camping trip. They had gone to bed and were lying there looking up at the sky. Holmes said, "Watson, look up. What do you see?"

"Well, I see thousands of stars."

"And what does that mean to you?"

"Well, I guess it means we will have another nice day tomorrow. What does it mean to you, Holmes?"

"Someone has stolen our tent."

152

Quote

Laugh and the world laughs with you.
Snore and you sleep alone.

JOKE

It was the grand opening for a business that had moved to a larger space. When one of the clients sent flowers for the occasion, the business owner was surprised by the message on the accompanying card—Rest in Peace.

When the owner contacted the client to thank him, he mentioned the obvious mix-up on the card. As soon as they hung up, the client called the florist and vented his displeasure.

After a moment's silence, the florist said, "You think you're angry. Imagine this. Somewhere there is a funeral today and they have a flower arrangement with a note saying, 'Congratulations on your new location.'"

BLOOPER

Marvin Tuttle has notified the church office that he lost his dog somewhere in the vicinity of Lake Charles. The dog is deaf and answers to the name of Thunder.

Quote

The simplest toy for a child to control is his grandparent.

JOKE

A fellow looked pretty worried when he arrived at the doctor's office for his annual physical. Noticing the patient's anxiety the doctor asked, "Is anything troubling you?"

"Well, to tell the truth, Doc, yes," replied the patient. "You see, I seem to be getting forgetful. No, actually, it's worse than that. I'm never sure where I put the car or whether I answered a letter or where I'm going or what it is I'm going to do once I get there, *if* I get there. I really need your help. What can I do?"

The doctor thought for a moment. "Pay me in advance."

154

Quote

Why do so many people think
they are the exception to the rule?

JOKE

An older man was getting prepped for surgery. Though
the surgery was minor, he insisted that his son, a
renowned surgeon, perform the operation. Just before the
anesthesia was administered, the patient asked to speak
to his son.

"Yes, Dad, what is it?"

"Don't be nervous. Do your best, and just remember
this: If something happens to me, your mother is going
to come and live with you and your wife."

155

Part 1
Irritations for a Sane Person

You have to try on a pair of sunglasses with that stupid little plastic thing hanging in the middle of your nose.

The person behind you in the supermarket line runs his cart into the back of your ankle.

There's always a car riding your tail when you're slowing down to find an address.

You open a can of soup and the lid falls in.

It's bad enough that you step in dog poop, but you don't realize it until you walk across your white living room rug.

The tiny red string on the Band-Aid wrapper breaks before you get the Band-Aid out.

Whatever you take out of a box can never be put back in the box exactly the same way.

Three hours and 3 meetings after lunch, you look in the mirror and see a piece of parsley stuck between your front teeth.

BLOOPER

Mark Anderson advanced to the 2nd round of the Reginal Spelling Bee.

Quote

When a man is wrapped up in himself,
he makes a very small package.

JOKES

You know you've had enough of this high-tech world when your kid says her Tinker Toys need more memory.

I encourage my children to read the newspaper, but they're holding out for a remote that turns the pages.

157

BLOOPER

Adult forum: Beginning the 1st Sunday of next month, Pastor Hodges will lead a 6-part series on the book of Genesis. Were Adam and Eve really naked in the Garden? Come see for yourself.

Quote

The ultimate test of fame is to have a crazy person believe he is you.

JOKE

When I was younger, I hated going to weddings. Invariably, after the wedding and during the reception, my grandmothers, my aunts, and any other female relatives would come up to me and poke me in the ribs, cackling, "You're next."

They finally stopped after I started doing the same thing to them at funerals!

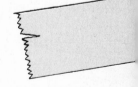

158

BLOOPER

We regret to announce that Associate Pastor Burns is leaving. He will resign next Friday.

Quote

Everything is funny as long as it happens to someone else.

JOKE

A less than fastidious wife was being teased good-naturedly by her husband. "You know, dear, I can write my name in the dust on the mantel."

To which she sweetly replied, "Yes, darling, I know. That's why I married a college graduate."

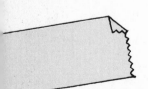

BLOOPER

The annual June board retreat will be held in June this year as opposed to July.

Quote

To the fool, a bright idea is beginner's luck.

JOKE

While waiting to see a new dentist, a woman noticed his diploma displayed in the waiting room. Reading the dentist's full name, she recalled a boy with that name in her high school class 40 years earlier. But as soon as she saw the dentist, she discarded the thought. This balding man with the deeply lined face was way too old to have been her classmate.

After the examination, she asked the dentist if he had attended the local high school.

"Yes," he replied.

"When did you graduate?"

"In 1957."

"Why, you were in my class!" she exclaimed.

He looked at her closely. "What did you teach?"

160
Corporate Lingo Clarified

Competitive salary: We remain competitive by paying less than our competitors.

Join our fast-paced company: We have no time to train you.

Must be deadline-oriented: You'll be 6 months behind schedule on your first day.

Some overtime required: Some time each night and some time each weekend.

Duties will vary: Anyone in the office can boss you around.

Seeking candidates with a wide variety of experience: You'll need it to replace 3 people who just left.

Problem-solving skills a must: You're walking into a company in perpetual chaos.

Good communication skills: Management communicates, you listen, figure out what they want, and do it.

BLOOPER

Found in the church parking lot: American flag.
You must be able to describe it to claim it.

Quote

Life makes more sense looking backward,
but it has to be lived forward first.

JOKE

Vacationing in Montana, a family drove past a building in a small town. Pointing to it, the mother told the children that it was a Baptist church.

"It must be a franchise," her 8-year-old son observed. "There's one back home just like it."

162

Quote

You have reached middle age when all you exercise is caution.

JOKE

One night a wife found her husband standing over their baby's crib. Silently, she watched him as he looked at the sleeping infant. Reflected on his face was a range of emotions—disbelief, doubt, delight, amazement, enchantment, skepticism.

Touched by this unusual display of deep and overt feelings, she slipped her arm around her husband's waist and said, with tear-filled eyes, "A penny for your thoughts."

"It's amazing!" he replied. "I just can't see how anybody can make a crib like that for only $46.50."

163

Quote

The easiest way to remain poor is to pretend to be rich.

JOKES

Teacher: George, go to the map and find North America.
George: Here it is!
Teacher: Correct. Now, class, who discovered America?
Class (in rousing unison): George!

Teacher: Tommy, why do you always get so dirty?
Tommy: Well, I'm a lot closer to the ground than you are.

164

BLOOPER

The women's guild heard Mrs. Elsa Border talk about planning for spontaneity.

Quote

It's easy to spot a well-informed man—
he's the one whose views match yours.

JOKE

A distraught patient phoned her doctor's office.

"Is it true," the woman asked the nurse, "that the medication the doctor prescribed is to be taken for the rest of my life?"

"Yes."

There was a moment of silence before the woman said, "I'm wondering, then, just how serious my condition is. This prescription is marked 'No Refills.'"

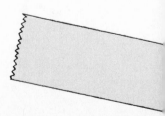

165 10/21/15

Life's Imponderables

Before they invented drawing boards, what did they go back to?

Does the Little Mermaid wear an algebra?

How do I set my laser printer on stun?

How is it possible to have a civil war?

If all the world is a stage, where is the audience sitting?

If love is blind, why is lingerie so popular?

If one synchronized swimmer drowns, do the rest have to drown too?

If the #2 pencil is the most popular, why is it still #2?

If you're born again, do you have two belly buttons?

If you ate pasta and antipasto, would you still be hungry?

If you try to fail, and succeed, which have you done?

BLOOPER

Sermon sign:
The Man Who Lived with Pigs. Dr. Alfred Ramsey.

Quote

The only thing improved by anger is
the arch on a cat's back.

JOKE

A mother was at the beach with her children when her
4-year-old son ran up to her, grabbed her hand, and led
her to the shore where a seagull lay dead in the sand.

"Mommy, what happened to him?" the little boy asked.

"He died and went to heaven."

"But why did God throw him back?"

BLOOPER

Tryouts will be held Wednesday for the Isadora High School summer softball team. All those interested over the age of 20 please attend.

Quote

A bore never runs out of conversation—just listeners.

JOKE

A young couple went on a cruise for their honeymoon. When they got back, the bride called her mother. "How was the honeymoon?" asked her mom.

"The honeymoon was fine," she replied. "But as soon as we returned to the apartment, he began using horrible language. Things I'd never heard before. Terrible 4-letter words. I want to come home!"

Alarmed, the mother asked, "What 4-letter words?"

"Dust, iron, wash, cook."

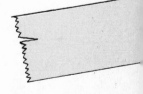

168

BLOOPER

Teaching students about the Bible raises their knowledge of the Bible, so claimed school superintendent Bailey.

Quote

You *can* move a mountain. Try doing it a stone at a time.

JOKE

A flight attendant noticed that a little girl traveling on her own was wearing a Medical Alert bracelet. The flight attendant asked her what the bracelet was for.

"I'm allergic to nuts and eggs."

"Are you allergic to cats too?"

"I don't know. I don't eat cats," the little girl replied.

BLOOPER

Gossip singing tonight at 6:00 with The Redemptions.

Quote

Most people would be satisfied with enough
if others didn't have more.

JOKE

An engineering student was walking on campus one day when a classmate rode up on a brand-new bicycle.

"Where did you get such a nice bike?"

"Well, yesterday I was walking along minding my own business when a beautiful woman rode up on this bike," his friend explained. "She threw the bike to the ground, took off her clothes, and said, 'Take what you want!'"

The second engineer nodded in approval. "Good choice. The clothes probably wouldn't have fit."

170

Part 1

What's with . . .

* What's with people who put carpeting on the lid of their toilet seat? Are they thinking, *Hmmm, if we have a party, there may not be enough standing room. I'd better carpet the toilet, too?*

* What's with hotels leaving a piece of chocolate on the pillow? When I woke up I thought my brain had leaked fecal matter.

* Have you ever noticed that the waiter who takes your order is not the one who brings your food anymore? What is that about? And which waiter are you tipping, anyway? The next time I go to a restaurant I'll just say, "Oh, sorry, I only eat the food. The guy who pays the bill will be along shortly."

* Would somebody please explain to me those signs that say, "No animals allowed except for Seeing Eye Dogs"? Who is that sign for? Is it for the dog, or the blind person?

* If airline seat cushions are such great flotation devices, why don't you ever see them at the beach?

BLOOPER

The Family Fest BBQ dinner will be a great place to lose your appetite.

Quote

Real friends are those who, after you've made a fool of yourself, don't think it did permanent damage.

JOKE

An archaeologist was digging in the Israeli desert and uncovered a casket containing a mummy. He called the curator of Jerusalem's natural history museum.

"I've just discovered a 3,000-year-old mummy of a man who died of heart failure!" the excited archaeologist exclaimed.

"Bring him in," the curator replied. "We'll check it out."

A week later, the amazed curator called the archaeologist. "You were right about the mummy's age and cause of death. How in the world did you know that?"

"Easy. There was a piece of paper in his hand that said, '10,000 shekels on Goliath.' "

172

BLOOPER

On their tour, Pastor Offet and his wife
saw places that no longer exist.

Quote

If at first you don't succeed,
try looking in the wastebasket for directions.

JOKE

A little boy was practicing the violin in the living room
while his father was trying to read in the den. The family
dog was lying quietly in the den, but when the screeching
sounds of the violin started, he began to howl loudly.

The father listened to the dog and the violin as long as
he could. Finally he yelled above the noise, "For heaven's
sake, can't you play something the dog doesn't know?"

BLOOPER

St. John's Scool boasts seveen merit scholarships.

Quote

No woman prefers a perfect husband,
because he doesn't give her anything to work on.

JOKE

An ancient monastery in Europe was perched high on a cliff several hundred feet in the air. The only way to reach the monastery was to ride in a basket that was pulled to the top by several monks. The view was both breathtaking and terrifying.

One tourist got exceedingly nervous about halfway up the cliff when he noticed that the rope holding the basket was extremely frayed. With a trembling voice, he asked the monk who was riding with him how often they replaced the rope.

"Whenever it breaks."

174

BLOOPER

Edwin Kaduce is looking for a home for his German
shepherd. The dog weighs 85 pounds, is neutered,
and speaks German.

Quote

If you think you might be able to look back at today and
laugh about it—why not do it today?

JOKE

A genie appeared during a university faculty meeting and
told the dean that in return for his unselfish, exemplary
behavior, he would be rewarded with his choice of infinite
wealth, wisdom, or beauty.

Without hesitating, the dean selected infinite wisdom.

"Done!" said the genie, and *poof!* disappeared.

All heads turned toward the dean, who was surrounded
by a faint halo of light.

One of his colleagues whispered, "Say something."

"I should have taken the money."

175

Part 2
What's with . . .

Why do they call it a "building"? It looks like they're finished. Why isn't it a "built"?

Why is it when you turn on the TV you see ads for telephone companies, and when you turn on the radio you hear ads for TV shows, and when you get put on hold on the phone you hear a radio station?

Why is it illegal to park in a handicapped parking space, but no one gives you a ticket when you use a handicapped stall in the bathroom?

How come you have to pay someone to rotate your tires? Isn't that the basic idea behind the wheel? Don't they rotate on their own?

You're sitting at a red light. When the car ahead of you pulls up a couple of inches, you do, too. You feel as if you've made real progress as you say to yourself, *Whew, I thought I'd be late, but now that I am 9 inches closer, I can stop for coffee and a doughnut!*

176

BLOOPER

There will be a free self-help group in the church fellowship hall on Wednesday evening at 7:00 for alcohol users who do not wish to change .

Quote

An optimist is one who gets chased up a tree by a lion but enjoys the scenery.

JOKE

A young fellow asked a rich, old businessman how he made his money. The man nodded sagely and said, "It was 1932, the depth of the Great Depression, and I was down to my last nickel.

"I invested that nickel in an apple that I polished all day. At the end of the day, I sold that shiny apple for 10 cents.

"The next morning, I invested those 10 cents in 2 apples. I spent the entire day polishing them and sold them for 20 cents. I continued this for a month and accumulated a fortune of $1.37."

"That's amazing," the young man said.

"Then my wife's father died and left us 2 million dollars."

BLOOPER

Pastor Wilson had been preaching for 40 years when he decided that he had said enough.

Quote

It is hard to believe that a fellow is telling the truth when you know that you would lie if you were in his place.

JOKES

Giraffiti: Vandalism painted very, very high.

Karmageddon: It's like, when everybody is sending off all these really bad vibes, right? And then, like, Earth explodes, and it's like, a serious bummer.

Dopeler Effect: The tendency for stupid ideas to seem smarter when they come at you rapidly.

BLOOPER

Meals on Wheels is looking for volunteers. You must like food preparation and be willing to get your hands dirty.

Quote

It takes less time to do the right thing
than to explain why you did it wrong.

JOKE

At a golf course, 4 men approached the 16th tee. The straight fairway lay along a road and a bike path, which were separated from the course by a fence.

The 1st golfer teed off and hooked the ball. The ball soared over the fence, bounced off the bike path onto the road, hit the tire of a moving bus, and was knocked back onto the fairway.

The other 3 golfers couldn't believe their eyes. Finally one asked, "How on earth did you do that?"

He shrugged and said, "You have to know the bus schedule."

BLOOPER

The St. Thomas women's jazzercise class will meet at 7 a.m. That way you'll be exercising before your brain figures out what you're doing.

Quote

Always look in the oven before you turn it on.

JOKE

A man shouted frantically into the phone, "My wife is pregnant, and her contractions are only 2 minutes apart!"
   "Is this her first child?" the doctor asked.
   "No!" the man shouted. "This is her husband!"

180

As a College Freshman You Wish You'd Known . . .

* that free food served at 10:00 is gone by 9:50;
* that dorms can be your lifeline and your personal hell at the same time;
* that Ramen noodles and spaghetti would keep you alive;
* how much you would miss your mother's washer and dryer;
* that you would no longer get an allowance;
* that every clock on campus displays a different time;
* that you would change so much and barely realize it;
* that home is a great place for regular visits.

181

BLOOPER

The youth group thanks everyone for supporting the car wash and wishes to apologize again to Rev. Oster. They really thought your windows were rolled up.

Quote

Last Father's Day my son gave me something I've always wanted—the keys to my car.

JOKE

I tell you, male drivers are a hazard to traffic. Driving to work this morning on the freeway, I looked over to my left, and there was this man doing 95 mph with his face up next to his rearview mirror—shaving!

I looked away for a couple seconds, and when I looked back, he was halfway in my lane. Scared me so bad I almost dropped my eyeliner pencil in my coffee!

182

BLOOPER

Pastor Nilquist insisted that as believers we have to walk the talk and not just talk from the hip.

Quote

Nothing needs reforming as much
as other people's habits.

JOKE

A middle-schooler was standing at his locker, holding his graded test. The big red F was hard to miss.

His best friend asked, "Why did you get such a low grade on that test?"

"Because of an absence," was the reply.

"You mean you were absent on the day of the test?"

"No, but the kid who sits next to me was."

BLOOPER

All the youth choirs of Our Redeemer Church
have been disbanded for the summer with the thanks
of the entire church.

Quote

The only time a fisherman tells the truth
is when he calls another fisherman a liar.

JOKE

A man was bitten by a stray, rabid dog. When his
neighbor checked to see how he was, the neighbor found
him writing frantically.

Thinking he was writing a will, the neighbor said, "You
know, rabies can be cured. You don't have to write a will
right now."

"Will? What will? I'm making a list of the people I
wanna bite!"

184

BLOOPER

All went well on the annual senior camping trip—despite temperatures in the late 40s and early 50s.

Quote

In golf, the ball always lies poorly and the golfer well.

JOKE

A mother was driving her 8-year-old daughter to her grandparents' home for an overnight stay. Traffic was unusually light, a far cry from what they normally encountered when driving to after-school activities during rush hour.

"Mom," the daughter began, "I have a question."

"Yes, honey?"

"When you're driving," the young girl asked, "are *you* ever the idiot?"

Part 4

Things My Mama Taught Me

My mama taught me about **behavior modification.**
Stop acting like your father!

My mama taught me about **envy.**
*There are millions of less fortunate children in this world
who don't have wonderful parents like you do!*

My mama taught me about **anticipation.**
Just wait until we get home.

My mama taught me about **receiving.**
You are going to get it when we get home!

My mama taught me about **wisdom.**
When you get to be my age, you will understand.

My mama taught me about **justice.**
*One day you'll have kids—and I hope they turn out
just like you!*

186

Quote

Inanimate objects are classified scientifically into 3 major categories—those that don't work, those that break down, and those that get lost.

JOKE

A man went to apply for a job. After completing the application, he waited anxiously as the human resources director read it.

Imagine his surprise when the HR director said, "We have an opening for people like you."

"Great!" he said excitedly. "What is it?"

"It's called the door!"

BLOOPER

If you don't believe in the organized church,
come to our church—we're as disorganized
as they come.

Quote

Show me a man with both feet on the ground,
and I'll show you a man who can't put his pants on.

JOKE

A man was still a little groggy from the anesthesia after
surgery. His wife was sitting at his bedside. As his eyes
fluttered open, he murmured, "You're beautiful." Then he
fell asleep.

A few hours later, he woke up, looked at his wife and
said, "You're cute."

"What happened to 'beautiful'?" she asked.

"I guess the drugs must be wearing off," he replied.

188

BLOOPER

Hymn: "Standing on the Premises of God."

Quote

He took his misfortune like a man.
He blamed it on his wife.

JOKE

A customer-service rep for a car rental company received a call from a driver who needed a tow. He was stranded on a busy highway, but he didn't know the make of the car he was driving.

The representative firmly asked again for a more detailed description of the car beyond "a blue 4-door."

"It's the one on fire."

BLOOPER

Edith Dother will speak to our Second Mile group at Grace Lutheran. She writes, "My husband lost 70 pounds of fat and kept it off for 3 years." She will bring samples.

Quote

If it weren't for the optimist, the pessimist would not know how happy he isn't.

JOKE

Long, long ago a Native American chief was about to die, so he called for Geronimo and Falling Rocks, the two bravest warriors in his tribe. The chief instructed each warrior to hunt buffalo. Whoever returned with the most buffalo skins would be chief.

About a month later Geronimo came back with 100 pelts, but sadly, Falling Rocks never returned.

Today as you drive through the West you can see evidence of the love and devotion the tribe had for this missing brave. At nearly every mile marker there are signs—Watch for Falling Rocks.

190

Have You Heard the One about . . .

A man sees a specialist about his medical problem. When the consultation is completed, the patient asks, "How much do I owe you?"

"My fee is $500," replies the physician.

"Five hundred dollars? That's highway robbery! No one charges that much!"

"In your case," the doctor replies, "I suppose I could adjust my fee to $200."

"Two hundred dollars? For one visit? Ridiculous."

"Well, then, could you afford $100?"

"Who has that kind of money?"

"Look," replies the doctor, growing irritated, "just give me 50 bucks and get out."

"I can give you $20," says the man. "Take it or leave it."

"I don't understand you," says the doctor. "Why did you choose the most expensive doctor in New York if you don't have any money?"

"Hey doc, when it comes to my health, nothing is too expensive."

BLOOPER

The church library is offering free kid rentals—hundreds of great ones to choose from.

Quote

Many people long for eternal life but cannot amuse themselves on a rainy evening.

JOKE

A man was reading the newspaper at the breakfast table. On the front page, he spotted a picture of a famous politician and his gorgeous wife.

Slightly jealous of the politician, the man said to his wife, "It's unfair that the biggest jerks in the world catch the most beautiful wives."

"Why, thank you, dear," his wife said with a smile.

192

BLOOPER

The Eden Valley Church softball team
improved their record to 0–3.

Quote

When it comes to getting a suntan, ignorance is blister.

JOKE

Two boys were talking during recess. "I'm really worried,"
said the 1st boy. "My dad works long hours to pay for all
the nice things I have. And when my mom comes home
from work, she spends her time cooking and cleaning."

"Sounds OK to me," said his friend. "What are you
worrying about?"

"What if they escape?"

193

Quote

No man needs a vacation as much as
the man who just had one.

JOKE

Two hefty men came to install a new kitchen floor in a woman's house. After moving the stove and refrigerator, the job went pretty quickly.

As the men were getting ready to leave, the woman asked them to move the heavy appliances back in place.

The two men demanded $45, stating it was not in their contract.

Disgruntled, the woman paid them. A minute after they left, however, the doorbell rang. It was the 2 men. "Your car is blocking our van," they gruffly informed the woman, "and we need you to move it."

"Sure," the woman said sweetly. "That will be $45 please."

194

Quote

Before giving someone a piece of your mind,
ask yourself: *Can I spare it?*

JOKE

A computer tech support person enjoyed chatting with his customers while waiting for their computers to reboot. One call for computer assistance came from a long-haul truck driver.

"I'd love to drive a big rig," the tech said, "but I'd worry about falling asleep at the wheel."

"Here's a tip to stay awake," the 18-wheeler driver offered. "Put a $100 bill in your left hand and hold it out the window."

195

Part 1
Yep, You're Living in the 2000s When . . .

* your reason for not staying in touch with family is that they do not have e-mail;

* you have a list of 15 phone numbers to reach your family of 3;

* your grandmother asks you to send her a JPEG file of your newborn so she can create a screen saver;

* you pull up in your own driveway and use your cell phone to see if anyone is home;

* every commercial on television has a Web site address at the bottom of the screen;

* you buy a computer and 3 months later it's obsolete and worth half the price you paid;

* leaving the house without your cell phone, which you didn't have the first 20 or 30 (or 60) years of your life causes sheer panic, and no matter how far you've driven, you turn around to retrieve it;

* using real money, instead of credit or debit, to buy something is both a hassle and takes planning.

196

Quote

The human brain is like a freight car—created to hold a large capacity but often running empty.

JOKE

A young businessman was sitting in the VIP lounge at an airport waiting for a client. Suddenly, the young man noticed Bill Gates sitting across the room.

He introduced himself to Gates, explaining that he was sealing an important business deal.

"Could you possibly throw a quick 'Hello, Chris' at me when I'm with my client?" he brashly asked Gates. Remembering how it was to start out, Gates agreed.

Five minutes after the client arrived, the young man felt a tap on his shoulder.

"Hey, Chris, what's happening?" asked Bill.

"Take a hike, Gates," the young man replied. "I'm in a meeting."

BLOOPER

Church newsletter classifieds: Fred Hectler of the SonShine Class has an American flag with 60 stars for sale, plus pole.

Quote

Children are like mosquitoes—the minute they stop making noise, they're into something.

JOKE

Five years after a couple were married, they received their final wedding gift—an ice-cream maker. In an attempt to cover procrastination with humor, the friend who sent it included a note: "I wanted to make sure the marriage would last."

The wife wasn't amused, but she thought the present deserved a thank-you note anyway, which she dutifully sent 5 years later. Her note read: "The ice-cream maker has lasted, too."

198

BLOOPER

Pastor Stewart complained that there are too many evangelicals on the Evangelical Mission to America committee.

Quote

When someone says, "It can't be done," they are actually saying, "I don't want to do it."

JOKE

A man followed a woman and her dog out of a movie theater. He stopped her and said, "I'm sorry to bother you, but I couldn't help noticing that your dog was really into the movie. He cried at the right spots and fidgeted in his seat at the boring parts. Most of all, he laughed like crazy at the funny parts. Did you find that unusual?"

"Yes," she replied, "because he hated the book!"

199

BLOOPER

The discount offered by the high school group's golf package is anywhere between 50% and half off.

Quote

Flattery is the art of telling people exactly what they think of themselves.

JOKE

The theme for the Vacation Bible School was "Discipleship and Saving Mother Earth," and the 4-year-old boy attending couldn't wait to tell his mother about the first day. "Mommy," he said excitedly, "we learned about Jesus and the 12 recycles."

200

Modern Inspirational Posters

If you do a good job and work hard, you may get a better job . . . someday.

The light at the end of the tunnel has been turned off due to budget cuts.

If you think we're a bad company, you should see our competition.

We put the *k* in *kwality*.

Hey! Two days without a human rights violation.

I love deadlines. Especially the whooshing sound they make as they go flying by.

We build great products when we feel like it and don't have any reason to call in sick.

Pride. Commitment. Teamwork. Words we use to get you to work for free.

BLOOPER

The Fulton County Humane Society is hosting their 4th annual beagle barbeque. Come on and join them in this unique event.

Quote

Don't ever count your chickens before they cross the road.

JOKES

In my day, we didn't have any rocks. We had to go down to the creek and wash our clothes by beating them with our heads.

Back in the 1970s we didn't have the space shuttle to get all excited about. We had to settle for men walking on the crummy moon.

BLOOPER

Elder and Police Chief Ricky Sawter reminded the congregation that their homes are safer if their doors are locked.

Quote

Ignorance is not hereditary—it's acquired.

JOKE

After the church service, a little boy said to the minister, "When I grow up, I'm going to give you some money."

"Well, thank you," the minister replied, "but why?"

"Because my daddy says you're one of the poorest preachers we've ever had."

203

BLOOPER

Bob Wilson has a hot tub for sale. It can comfortably sear 5 adults at a time.

Quote

Some people drink deeply at the fountain of knowledge—others only gargle.

JOKE

You've heard of Vincent Van Gogh's family, right?
  His obnoxious brother, Please Gogh.
  His brother who ate prunes, Gotta Gogh.
  His brother who worked in the convenience store,
    Stopn Gogh.
  His grandfather from Yugoslavia, U Gogh.
  His brother who bleached his clothes white, Hue Gogh.
  His cousin from Illinois, Chicaw Gogh.

204

Quote

A fool and his money will always have a lot of girlfriends.

JOKE

Here's the rest of Van Gogh's clan:

His uncle, the magician, Wherediddy Gogh.

His cousin from Mexico, Amee Gogh.

His Mexican cousin's American half brother, Grin Gogh.

His nephew who drove a stagecoach for a living, Wellsfar Gogh.

His constipated uncle, Cant Gogh.

His ballroom dancing aunt, Tang Gogh.

205

You'll Never Hear This from a Consultant . . .

You're right; I'm billing way too much for this.

Bet you I can go a week without saying "synergy" or "value-added."

How about paying me based on the success of the project?

This whole strategy is based on a Harvard business case I read.

Actually, the only difference is that I charge more than they do.

I don't know enough to speak intelligently about that.

Implementation? I only care about writing long reports.

I can't take the credit. It was Ed in your marketing department.

The problem is, you have too much work for too few people.

Everything looks okay to me.

BLOOPER

Mark your calendars for July 12. Our annual church picnic will begin at Waggoner Park at noon. In case of rain, meet at 10 under the tarp by the bandstand.

Quote

Never go to bed angry. Stay up and fight.

JOKE

A man, waiting for his flight to New York, heard the announcement that a flight to Las Vegas was full. The airline was looking for volunteers to give up their seats. In exchange, the airline was giving a $100 voucher for the next flight and a first-class seat on the flight leaving an hour later.

Immediately, 8 people ran up to the counter. The observer was surprised when seconds later all 8 people sat down grumpily. The reason became clear when the ticket counter person announced, "If there is anyone *other* than the flight crew who'd like to volunteer, please step forward."

BLOOPER

Pastor Ralph Simmons said his favorite overseas destination is Canada.

Quote

The one thing you can do better than anyone else is read your own handwriting.

JOKE

A father was picking up his son's preschool friend for summer swim lessons. As the friend left the house, the dad noticed an older woman hugging him.

"Is that your grandmother?" he asked when the boy got in the car.

"Yes, she's visiting us for a few weeks."

"That's nice. Where does she live?"

"At the airport. Whenever we want her, we just go out there and get her."

208

Quote

There is nothing wrong with having nothing to say unless you say it aloud.

JOKE

An atheist was out fishing when suddenly his boat was attacked by the Loch Ness monster. The beast tossed him and his boat high in the air. Then it opened its mouth, ready to swallow both whole.

Sailing head-over-heels, the man cried out, "Oh, my God! Help me!"

Amazingly, the boat got wedged in the monster's mouth as the atheist hung on for dear life. Then a booming voice came from above. "I thought you didn't believe in me!"

"Come on, God, give me a break!" the man pleaded. "Two minutes ago I didn't believe in the Loch Ness monster either!"

BLOOPER

Raymond Wilson has a free air conditioner.
It runs, but it doesn't cool.

Quote

If the devil catches you idle, he'll soon put you to work.

JOKE

"Just to establish some parameters," said the professor,
"Mr. Tarr, what is the opposite of joy?"
   "Sadness," said the student.
   "And the opposite of depression, Ms. Helms?"
   "Elation."
   "And you, Mr. Fields, how about the opposite of woe?"
   "I believe that would be giddy up!"

Part 2

Irritations for a Sane Person

* You drink from a soda can and discover someone has used it for an ashtray.

* You slice your tongue licking an envelope.

* Your tire gauge lets out half the air while you're trying to get a reading.

* A radio station comes in perfectly when you're standing near the radio, but it buzzes, drifts in and out, and spits every time you move away.

* There are always 1 or 2 ice cubes you have to wrestle out of the tray.

* You wash a garment with a tissue in the pocket, and your entire laundry comes out covered with teeny tiny specks of tissue.

* The car behind you blasts its horn because you let a pedestrian finish crossing.

* A nearly undetectable piece of foil candy wrapper hits your filling.

* You set the alarm on your digital clock for 7 p.m. instead of 7 a.m.

* The deejay on the radio doesn't tell you who sang that song.

BLOOPER

Susan Howell, children's ministry director, has this tip for new parents. "Show your children that you care. Start off by learning each of their names."

Quote

Almost everyone knows the difference between right and wrong, but some hate to make the decision.

JOKE

Although the couple was being married in New Hampshire, the bride wanted to add a touch of her home state, Kansas, to the wedding. Explaining this to a friend, her fiancé said that instead of throwing rice after the ceremony, the plan was to throw grains of wheat.

To which the friend replied in a serious tone, "It's a good thing she's not from Idaho."

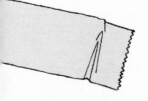

212

Quote

Now I'm confused—
my fortune cookie just contradicted my horoscope.

JOKE

Harvesting the usual bumper crop of squash, I took a bagful to the office. I piled them on the table in the break room with a sign: Free Zucchini.

   The next day I noticed an addition to my sign. Below "Free Zucchini," someone had written, "Save the Whales."

213

Quote

My boss continues to confuse bad management
with destiny.

JOKE

A teenage girl brought her new boyfriend home to meet her parents. They were appalled by his appearance: leather jacket, tattoos, and multiple piercings.

Later, the parents pulled their daughter aside and expressed their concern. "Dear," said the mother diplomatically, "he doesn't seem very nice."

"Oh, please, Mom," replied the daughter in exasperation. "If he wasn't nice, why would he be doing 500 hours of community service?"

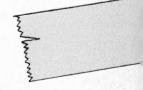

214

BLOOPER

After 25 years of dedicated service to Reedsville Methodist Church, the congregation proudly presented Pastor Hyams with a new Rolodex watch.

Quote

An optimist is one who believes that the fly in the car is looking for a way to get out.

JOKES

Q: How do crazy people go through the forest?
A: They take the psycho path.

Q: Why do bagpipers walk when they play?
A: They're trying to get away from the noise.

Q: Why do gorillas have big nostrils?
A: Because they have big fingers.

215

Training for the Tour de France?

A man decided to bike from Phoenix to Flagstaff. He was feeling confident until the road began getting steeper, climbing to 7,000 feet. When his legs finally gave out, he knew he needed to turn back.

Hoping to hitch a ride at least part of the way home, he stood on the side of the highway. An hour later a guy in a Corvette pulled over and offered him a ride. Because the bike wouldn't fit in the car, the driver found a piece of rope and said, "I'll tie one end of the rope to the bumper of the car and the other end of the rope to your bike." The cyclist was game. Before getting in the car, the driver gave one more instruction: "If I go too fast, honk your bike horn, and I'll slow down."

Everything went fine for the first 30 miles. Suddenly, another Corvette blew past them. Forgetting about his "passenger" in the back, the first Corvette driver hit the accelerator. Within minutes, the Corvettes blew through a speed trap.

The state patrolman radioed to a patrol car ahead of the racing cars: "Two Corvettes heading your way, clocked at over 120 mph."

Then he added, "And you're not going to believe this, but there's guy on a bike behind them honking to pass."

216

Quote

There was no respect for youth when I was young, and now that I am old, there is no respect for age—I missed it coming and going.

JOKE

A country preacher decided to skip Sunday services to go bear hunting. As he rounded the trail, he and a bear collided, sending the preacher tumbling down the mountainside. His rifle flew one way and he flew the other, breaking both legs when he landed. Unfortunately, the bear was charging straight at him.

"Oh, Lord," the preacher prayed. "Forgive me for skipping church today. Please grant me one wish—make a Christian out of that bear."

That very instant, the bear skidded to a halt, fell to its knees, and began to pray, "Dear God, bless this food I am about to receive."

BLOOPER

Students on the day trip to Chicago will enjoy gourmet sandwiches made with American French bread.

Quote

When you start to look like your passport picture, you know you need a vacation.

JOKE

A family was hosting a dinner for the minister and his family of 10. At the table, the hostess turned to her 6-year-old daughter and said, "Would you like to say the blessing?"

"I don't know what to say," she replied.

"Just say what you hear Mommy say."

The youngster bowed her head and said, "Dear Lord, why on earth did I invite all these people to dinner?"

218

BLOOPER

For the youth fund-raiser, Lance Ransom of Ransom Farms in Pine Grove is offering Georgia peaches—grown in California—at 89 cents per pound.

Quote

Size may not matter all that much. The whale is endangered, but the ant is doing just fine.

JOKE

A woman's coworkers sympathized as she complained that her back was really sore from moving furniture.

"Why didn't you wait until your husband got home?" someone asked her.

"I could have," she said, "but the couch is easier to move if he's not on it."

BLOOPER

The church custodian asks guests to refrain from throwing lice at the bride and groom. It's hard to clean up, and the birds won't eat it.

Quote

It is easy to start a fire by rubbing 2 sticks together—if one of them happens to be a match.

JOKE

Two guys were late for the baseball game, so when they finally found a parking place, jumped out of the car and locked it, the driver realized too late that he had left the keys in the ignition.

"Why don't we get a coat hanger to open it?" his friend suggested.

"That won't work. People will think we're trying to break in to steal the car."

"Well," his helpful friend said. "We'd better think of something fast. It's starting to rain, and the sunroof is open!"

220

And the Verdict Is . . .

A man was on trial for murder. There was strong evidence against him, but the victim's body had never been found. The defendant's lawyer, knowing that his client would probably be convicted, stood before the jury for his closing statement.

"Ladies and gentlemen of the jury, I have a surprise. Within one minute, the person presumed dead in this case will walk into this courtroom." He looked at the courtroom door. The jurors followed his glance. A minute passed but nothing happened.

"Actually, I made that scenario up," the lawyer confessed. "But every one of you looked at the door because you have reasonable doubt as to whether there is a victim in this case. I insist that you return a verdict of not guilty."

The jury, clearly confused, left to deliberate. A few minutes later, they returned and pronounced a guilty verdict.

"I don't understand," the lawyer said. "I saw all of you stare at the door."

"Yes, everyone looked," the jury foreman explained. "Everyone, that is, except your client."

BLOOPER

Bring your appetites to the annual all-church rot dog roast. Utensils and charcoal provided.

Quote

Anybody can give advice—
the trouble comes in finding someone
interested in using it.

JOKE

A man called an airline's reservation line to book a flight. Taking down the credit card information, the service representative asked him, "Would you please spell the name as it appears on the card, sir?"

"V-I-S-A."

222

BLOOPER

Sunday school students are scheduled to hear John the
Baptist lecture.

Quote

When people tell you how young you look,
they are also telling you how old you are.

JOKE

A couple touring Florida stopped at a rattlesnake farm.

"Don't you ever get bitten by snakes?" the tourist asked
the snake handler.

"On rare occasions."

"What do you do when you're bitten by a snake?"

"I always carry a razor-sharp knife in my pocket. As
soon as I'm bitten, I make deep criss-cross marks across
the bite and suck the poison from the wound."

"What would happen if you accidentally sat on a
rattler?" persisted the woman.

"Ma'am," answered the snake handler, "that will be the
day I learn who my real friends are."

BLOOPER

Church newsletter classifieds: For sale—old dresses from grandmother in really great condition.

Quote

Creditors have better memories than lenders.

JOKE

In medieval times there was a baker's assistant in charge of preparing and pouring the dough mixture for the sausage rolls or, as the king called them, "wurst rolls." Because people back then were identified by their professions, he was known as Richard the Pourer.

One day Richard ran out of the special spice he used in the batter. He called his apprentice and sent him to the store to buy more. At the store, the apprentice forgot the name of the ingredient. Hoping that the storekeeper might know what spice it was, he said, "It's for Richard the Pourer, for batter for wurst."

224

BLOOPER

Forty percent of the children in our under-12 Sunday school classes are under 12, up from 30 percent last year.

Quote

One good thing about kids—they seldom go around showing pictures of their grandparents.

JOKE

Q: What do you call an Irishman who keeps bouncing off walls?
A: Rick O'Shea.

Q: Why can't you borrow money from a leprechaun?
A: Because they're always a little short.

Q: What do you get from a pampered cow?
A: Spoiled milk.

225

Have You Heard the One about . . .

A man received a parrot for his birthday. The parrot was fully grown, with a bad attitude and a worse vocabulary. Every other word was an expletive. Those that weren't expletives were downright rude. The new owner tried to change the bird's attitude with soft music and soothing conversations but nothing worked.

Frustrated, the man yelled at the bird and the bird yelled back. He shook the bird and the bird tried to bite him. Finally, in a moment of desperation, the man stuffed the parrot in the freezer.

For a few moments he heard the bird squawk and kick and scream. Then suddenly there was quiet. Not a sound for half a minute. Fearing that he might have hurt the bird, the owner quickly opened the freezer door. The parrot calmly stepped out and said, "I believe I may have offended you with my rude language and actions. I will endeavor at once to correct my behavior. I really am sorry and beg your forgiveness."

At first astonished by the bird's change in attitude, the man clearly understood what had caused the reversal when the parrot said: "May I ask what the chicken did?"

226

Quote

I have 2 wonderful children. Two out of 5 isn't bad.

JOKES

Funny signs:

In a clothing store: Great bargains for men with 16 and 17 necks.

In an airline ticket office: We take your bags and send them in all directions.

On a long-established dry cleaners: Thirty-eight years on the same spot.

BLOOPER

Come to Briargate Valley Church's re-creation of colonial America. Witness an authentic hanging and witch-burning.

Quote

The problem with 2nd opinions is that's exactly how long most people think before offering them.

JOKES

One million microphones: One megaphone

One million bicycles: Two megacycles

Two thousand mockingbirds: Two kilomockingbirds

Ten cards: One decacards

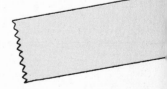

228

BLOOPER

Pastor Criswell encouraged the congregation not to be afraid of challenges. "If you want to go out in the rain, you have to be prepared to get burned."

Quote

I have a pocket comb—but then,
who wants to comb pockets?

JOKE

You know it's going to be a bad day when your teenager knocks on your bedroom door first thing in the morning and says, "Today is Nerd Day at school, Dad. Can I borrow some of your clothes?"

BLOOPER

The Adams Road nudist camp must be watched, Pastor Higgens stated at the recent board meeting.

Quote

Everyone wanted him to run for Congress. They figured it was the best way to get him out of town.

JOKE

A farmer's barn burned down, and his wife called the insurance company. "We had that barn insured for $50,000," she said. "I want my money."

"Insurance doesn't work quite like that," the agent replied. "We will ascertain the value of what was insured and provide you with a new barn of comparable worth."

There was a long pause before the farmer's wife said, "Then I'd like to cancel the policy on my husband."

230

Part 2

Yep, You're Living in the 2000s When . . .

* you just tried to enter your password on the microwave;
* you consider second-day air delivery painfully slow;
* your dining room table is now your flat filing cabinet;
* your idea of being organized is multiple-colored Post-it notes;
* you hear most of your jokes via e-mail instead of in person;
* you get an extra phone line so you can get phone calls;
* you disconnect from the Internet and get this awful feeling, as if you just pulled the plug on a loved one;
* you get up in the morning and go online before getting your coffee;
* you wake up at 2 a.m. to go to the bathroom, and on your way back to bed you check your e-mail;
* you start tilting your head sideways to smile;
* you're reading this and nodding and laughing;
* even worse, you know exactly who you are going to forward this to!

BLOOPER

From a church bulletin: Presentation of our Ties and Offerings

Quote

Anyone can deal with a crisis—it's this day-to-day grind that wears you out.

JOKE

NASA was screening 3 candidates for a one-way trip to Mars. The interviewer asked the first applicant, an engineer, how much he wanted to be paid for going. "One million dollars," the engineer said, "all to be donated to my alma mater—MIT."

The next applicant, a doctor, was asked the same question. "Two million dollars," the doctor said. "I want to give a million to my family and leave the other million for the advancement of medical research."

The final applicant, a lawyer, beat the interviewer to the punch when he whispered, "If you give me 3 million, I'll give you 1 million, I'll keep a million, and we'll send the engineer."

232

BLOOPER

The elders voted 6 to 5 that we have our church participate in Unity Sunday.

Quote

Business is like a wheelbarrow—
it stands still until someone pushes it.

JOKE

A sign in an office window read: *Help wanted. Must type 70 words a minute, be computer literate, and bilingual. An equal opportunity employer.*

A dog grabbed the sign and walked into the manager's office. Laughing, the man said, "I can't hire a dog."

The dog pointed to the line: *An equal opportunity employer.* So the manager said, "Okay, type this letter."

The dog sat down at the computer and a minute later completed a perfectly formatted letter.

"OK. Now write a computer program for it and run it." The dog completed the task in 15 minutes.

"That's great, but you're not bilingual."

"Meow."

BLOOPER

Steve Marlowe will present a talk on Charles Darwin in the Fellowship Hall. Darwin wrote the book *The Organ of the Species.*

Quote

The only thing harder than sticking to a diet
is keeping quiet about it.

JOKE

An astronomer was trekking through the African jungle looking for the ideal location to observe a total eclipse of the sun when, suddenly, he was captured by cannibals. Thinking quickly, he decided to pose as a god and threaten to extinguish the sun if he was not released. Since the eclipse was happening the next day, the timing had to be perfect. So he asked his guard when they planned to kill him.

"Intruders are always killed when the sun reaches the highest point in the sky on the day after their capture."

"Great," the astronomer replied, thinking he was set.

"But in your case," the guard continued, "we're going to wait until after the eclipse."

234

BLOOPER

Good news! After the accident, they x-rayed Pastor Jim's head and found nothing.

Quote

It isn't what's on the table that matters as much as what's on the chairs.

JOKE

A new bride called her mother in tears. "Oh, Mom, I tried to make Grandma's meatloaf dinner tonight, and it's just awful! I followed the recipe you gave me, but it just didn't come out right. What could have gone wrong?"

"Let's go through the recipe together, honey," her mother said, trying to calm her down. "Read it out loud and we'll figure out what happened."

"Okay," the bride sniffled. "It starts out, 'Take 50 cents worth of ground beef . . .' "

235

Laws of Parenting

* The later you stay up, the earlier your child will wake up the next morning.

* For a child to become clean, something else must become dirty.

* Toys multiply to fill any space available.

* The longer it takes you to make a meal, the less your child will like it.

* Yours is always the only child who doesn't behave.

* If the shoe fits—it's expensive.

* The surest way to get something done is to tell a child not to do it.

* The gooier the food, the more likely it is to end up on the carpet.

* Backing the car out of the driveway causes your child to have to go to the bathroom.

* The more challenging the child, the more rewarding it is to be a parent . . . sometimes.

236

BLOOPER

The board of elders debated how to amateurize the cost of the new copier over its expected lifetime.

Quote

Make 3 correct guesses consecutively and you will have established yourself as an expert.

JOKE

A mother decided to stop worrying about her teenage son's driving; instead, she took advantage of it. She bought a "How's my driving?" bumper sticker with a 900 number on it.

At 50 cents a call, she's been making $38 a week.

BLOOPER

The church council approved the purchase of new snivel chairs for the pastor's office and study.

Quote

It is amazing how nice people are to you when they know you are going away.

JOKE

A hospital posted a notice in the nurse's lounge: "Remember, the first 5 minutes of a human being's life are the most dangerous."

Underneath, a nurse had written: "The last 5 are pretty risky, too."

238

Quote

The skin you love to touch—Dad's old pigskin wallet.

JOKE

The Sunday school teacher was describing how Lot's wife looked back and turned into a pillar of salt.

"My mommy looked back once while she was driving," a boy interrupted excitedly. "She turned into a telephone pole!"

BLOOPER

Come to church next Friday night. Pastor Williams will debate noted atheist Charles Downs. This is their 3rd face-to-face face-off.

Quote

I did not attend his funeral;
I sent a nice note saying I approved of it, however.

JOKE

A lawyer had had a little bit too much to drink, and on his way home he rear-ended the car in front of him. The lawyer got out of his car, walked over to the driver of the other car, and said, "Boy, are you in trouble! I'm a lawyer!"

"No, you're in trouble," the other driver said. "I'm a judge."

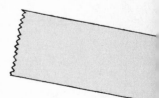

240

Kids' Kitchen Terms

Boil: The point a parent reaches upon hearing the automatic "Yuck" before a food is even tasted.

Casserole: Combination of favorite foods that go uneaten because they are mixed together.

Dessert: The reason for eating a meal.

Evaporate: Magic trick performed by children when it comes time to clear the table or wash dishes.

Fruit: A natural sweet not to be confused with dessert.

Refrigerator: A very expensive and inefficient room air conditioner when not being used as an art gallery.

Soda pop: Shake 'n' Spray.

Table leg: Percussion instrument.

BLOOPER

The public health nurses will be at the fellowship hall next Wednesday. They say the new vaccine may contain the flu this year.

Quote

Everyone likes a kidder, but no one lends him money.

JOKE

A man walked into an empty bar. The bartender, washing glasses behind the counter said, "I'll be with you in a minute. Help yourself to the peanuts."

Grabbing a handful of peanuts, the man heard someone say, "That's a sharp suit you're wearing." The guy looked around but no one was there.

He took another handful of peanuts and a voice said, "And that tie goes really well with it."

By now the guy was really baffled.

When the bartender came over, the guy whispered, "Where are those voices coming from?"

"Oh, I forgot to tell you," the bartender replied. "The peanuts are complimentary."

242

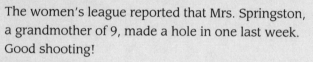

BLOOPER

The women's league reported that Mrs. Springston, a grandmother of 9, made a hole in one last week. Good shooting!

Quote

Humor can be dissected like a frog, but both of them die in the process.

JOKE

The Olympic skier Picabo Street is not only a world class athlete but also a nurse.

Working in the intensive care unit of a large metropolitan hospital, she was asked not to answer the telephone. It caused too much confusion when she said, "Picabo, ICU."

BLOOPER

The students performed music from the Taco Bell Cannon.

Quote

I thought my group insurance plan was great until I found out that I couldn't collect unless the whole group is sick.

JOKE

A blonde was crying her eyes out at work. "What's the matter?" her boss asked. The blonde replied, "Early this morning I got a phone call saying that my grandmother had passed away."

"Go ahead and take the rest of the day off," her boss said.

"Thanks, but I need to keep my mind occupied," the blonde said gratefully.

A few hours passed and the boss decided to check up on her. Once again the woman was crying hysterically. "Did something else happen?" he asked.

"I just hung up with my sister," she said between sobs. "Her grandmother died too!"

244

Quote

Income is something you can't live without or within.

JOKE

I went to the store the other day, and when I came out
5 minutes later, a cop was writing a parking ticket. "Come
on, officer," I said. "How about giving a guy a break?"

He ignored me and finished writing the ticket. So I
called him a piece of horse manure.

He whipped out a 2nd ticket and put it on the windshield with the 1st. Then he started writing a 3rd ticket!

This went on for another few minutes. The more I
verbally abused him, the more tickets he wrote. I didn't
care. My car was parked around the corner.

245

Preaching Really Hard

During an impassioned sermon on death and final judgment, the pastor said forcefully, "Each member of this church is going to die and face judgment." Glancing down at the front pew, he noticed a man with a big smile on his face.

The minister repeated his point louder. "Each member of this church is going to die and face judgment!" The man nodded and smiled even more.

This really got the preacher wound up. He pounded the pulpit emphatically when he came to the ultimatum: "Each member of this church is going to die and face judgment." Though everyone else in the congregation was looking somber, the man in front continued to smile.

Finally the preacher stepped off the platform, stood in front of the man and shouted, "I said each member of this church is going to die!" The man grinned from ear to ear.

After the service was over, the preacher made a beeline for the man. "I don't get it," the preacher said in frustration. "Whenever I said, 'Each member of this church is going to die,' your smile got bigger. Why?"

"I'm not a member of this church," the man replied.

246

BLOOPER

In their seminar, the Byrds claimed that living together is linked to divorce.

Quote

Love is blind, but marriage restores its sight.

JOKES

Resumé Oops:

Here are my qualifications for you to overlook.

Instrumental in ruining an entire franchise operation.

Experienced supervisor, defective with both rookies and seasoned professionals.

It's best for employers that I not work with people.

247

BLOOPER

Lt. Cassidy from the city police department said that police officers will begin to run down jaywalkers in front of the church unless they cross at the crosswalks.

Quote

When a man steals your wife, there is no better revenge than to let him keep her.

JOKE

The Sunday school lesson was about how God is personally interested in each one of us. At the end of class the teacher asked her students to write a letter to God during the week and bring it back the next Sunday. One little boy wrote: "Dear God, We had a good time at church today. Wish you could have been there."

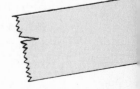

248

BLOOPER

Please remember John Perkins, a firefighter who hurt himself while distinguishing a fire last week.

Quote

Marriage halves our sadness, doubles our joy, and quadruples our expenses.

JOKE

A restaurant owner was convinced that his bouncer was the strongest man around. Hand the bouncer a lemon and he would squeeze it dry. "I'll give $1,000 to anyone who can squeeze out one more drop of juice," the owner announced.

There were numerous attempts, but nobody could do it. One day, a scrawny little man came in and asked to try.

The bouncer grabbed a lemon and crushed it with his bare hand before handing the rind to his competitor.

The scrawny man clenched his fist around the lemon and 20 drops fell into the glass!

"How'd you do that?" the owner asked the winner, counting out the money.

"I work for the IRS."

BLOOPER

Frank Mueller, city engineer, told the adult Sunday school class that the recent brown city water is safe to drink.

Quote

The most difficult year of marriage is the one you're in.

JOKE

Two buddies, Ray and Ed, were diehard baseball fans. One day they made a pact: Whoever died first would come back and tell his buddy if there was baseball in heaven.

One summer night, Ray died in his sleep. A few nights later, Ed heard a voice from beyond. "Ray, is that you?" Ed asked.

"Of course it's me," Ray replied.

"So tell me, Ray, is there baseball in heaven?"

"Well, I have good news and bad news. The good news is that there is baseball in heaven, Ed."

"That's wonderful! So what's the bad news?"

"You're pitching tomorrow night."

250

A Cat's Heaven

St. Peter is standing at heaven's pearly gates when a cat shows up. "You were a loving cat on earth," says St. Peter, "so I want to give you one special thing you have always wanted."

"Well, I did always want a nice satin pillow like my master had, so I could lie on it."

"That's easy," St. Peter replied. "We will have a satin pillow ready for you."

Next a family of mice appears at the pearly gates. St. Peter says, "Ah, I remember you. You were good mice on earth. You didn't steal food from anyone's house and never hurt other animals. Therefore, I want to grant you one special wish."

The father mouse replies, "Well, we always watched the children skating, and it looked like fun. Could we each have some skates, please?"

"Granted. You shall have your wish."

The next day, St. Peter saw the cat sunning itself on the pillow. "Well, cat, how's the satin pillow?"

"Absolutely wonderful," the cat replied. "And say, those 'Meals on Wheels' were an extra nice touch too!"

BLOOPER

The premarital workshop on Tuesday night will be followed by a grief recovery group.

Quote

The really frightening part about being middle-aged is the fact that you'll grow out of it.

JOKE

During a children's sermon, the pastor asked the children what *Amen* means. A little boy's hand immediately shot up: "Tha-tha-tha-that's all folks!"

252

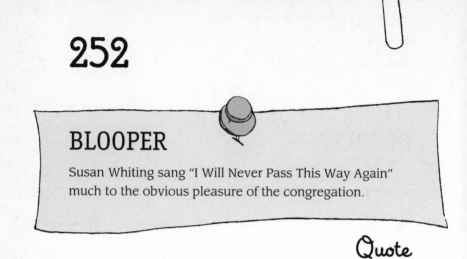

BLOOPER

Susan Whiting sang "I Will Never Pass This Way Again" much to the obvious pleasure of the congregation.

Quote

Don't promote a man who hasn't made some big mistakes—it's an indication that he hasn't done much.

JOKE

A student was asked to list the Ten Commandments in any order. His answer? "3, 6, 1, 8, 4, 5, 9, 2, 10, 7."

BLOOPER

A congregational-approved measure for congregational approval does not require a congregational vote by the congregation.

Quote

If you want to know what God thinks about money, look at the people he gives it to.

JOKE

A little boy needed $100 for a school field trip, so his mother told him to ask God for it. He prayed for 2 weeks, but nothing turned up. So he decided to ask God for the money in a letter.

At the post office, the postmaster opened the letter to God and decided to forward it to the President of the United States.

The President was charmed, so he told his secretary to send the boy $5. After receiving the money, the boy wrote a thank-you letter to God.

"Dear God, Thank you very much for sending the money. I noticed that you had to send it through Washington. As usual, those guys deducted $95. Thanks anyway!"

254

BLOOPER

Anna Freisen of Kansas City and Anna Dickerson of Tulsa visited Betty Leaky. The two Annas ate Betty's first cousin.

Quote

God likes common-looking people.
That's why he made so many of them.

JOKE

In his class lecture, a linguistics professor was explaining the double negative.

"In English, a double negative forms a positive. In some languages, though, such as Russian, a double negative is still a negative. However," he pointed out, "there is no language wherein a double positive can form a negative."

A voice from the back of the room piped up, "Yeah, right."

255

Part 2

Dictionary for Women

* Grocery list: What you spend half an hour writing, then forget to take with you to the store.

* Hairdresser: Someone who is able to create a style you will never be able to duplicate again.

* Hardware store: Similar to a black hole in space—if he goes in, he isn't coming out anytime soon.

* Lipstick: On your lips it's a color to enhance your mouth. On his collar it's a color only a tramp would wear.

* Park: Before children, a verb meaning "to go some-where and neck." After children, a noun meaning a place with a swing set and slide.

* Patience: The most important ingredient for dating, marriage, and children. See also *Tranquilizers*.

* Valentine's Day: A day when you have dreams of a candlelight dinner, diamonds, and romance, but consider yourself lucky to get a card.

* Waterproof mascara: Comes off if you cry, shower, or swim, but never when you want to remove it.

BLOOPER

Elmer and Cheryl Beumer of our sister congregation in Maysville have opened a new restaurant specializing in vegetarian cuisine, including lamb, beef, and chicken.

Quote

Some of the best reasons I ever found for remaining at the bottom of the corporate ladder are the people at the top.

JOKE

A wealthy man was looking for a birthday gift for his daughter. One day he spotted a beautiful white horse in a field. He found out that the owner had fallen on hard times, so he offered the man $500 for the horse. "I don't know, mister. It don't look so good," the owner said.

"How about $1,000?" The man gave the same response.

"Okay, I'll pay you $5,000 for the horse, and I won't take no for an answer," the father said. The owner agreed.

The daughter loved her present. But the first time she rode the horse, it ran into a tree. The father rushed back to the owner, demanding an explanation.

"I told you it don't look so good," he said truthfully.

BLOOPER

Church newsletter classifieds: For sale—free puppies (part Spitz, Datsun, and Pekingese).

Quote

When you hire people who are smarter than you are, you prove you are smarter than they are.

JOKE

A widow married a widower. Soon after the marriage she met a friend for lunch. "Does your husband ever talk about his first wife?" her friend asked.

"Not anymore, he doesn't," the widow replied.

"What stopped him?"

"I started talking about my next husband."

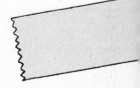

258

BLOOPER

At the denominational plenary session,
the bishop once again stated that teen pregnancy
drops sharply after age 25.

Quote

No one feels worse
than the person who gets sick on his day off.

JOKE

A man was driving along a rural road one day when he
saw a 3-legged chicken. Amazingly, he clocked the fowl
running at 20 miles per hour. He accelerated to 30 mph;
the chicken did too! The man sped up again; to his
surprise, the chicken passed him and ran down a
driveway.

The man saw a farmer surrounded by dozens of
3-legged chickens. He called out, "How did you get all
3-legged chickens?"

"I started breeding them because my wife, son, and I all
love to eat chicken legs."

"That's amazing!" said the driver "How do they taste?"

"Don't know. Haven't been able to catch any of them."

BLOOPER

At the All Saints workday, lunch will be provided,
so bring gloves and a shovel.

Quote

Teenagers express a burning desire to be different
by all dressing alike.

JOKE

Two young golfers were trying out a new course. The 1st
golfer sliced his ball into a wooded ravine. Grabbing his
8-iron, he proceeded down the embankment looking for
his ball.

In the thick underbrush he spotted something shiny.
As he got closer, he realized that the shiny object was an
8-iron in the hands of a skeleton, which was lying near
an old golf ball.

Shouting to his partner, he said, "Hey, come and look.
I have big trouble down here."

The 2nd golfer ran to the edge of the embankment and
called down, "What's the matter?"

A nervous voice answered. "Throw me my 7-iron.
Looks like you can't get out of here with an 8-iron."

260
Stranded

A multimillionaire was enjoying an afternoon on his yacht in the Caribbean when a severe storm hit. The near-hurricane force winds produced gigantic waves that eventually swamped and sank the yacht. It sank without a trace. The yacht owner and his chauffeur, the only two people on board, managed to swim to the closest island.

Lying exhausted on the deserted beach, the chauffeur began to panic. "We'll never be rescued!" But the multimillionaire just smiled.

"How can you be so calm?!" screamed the chauffeur, working himself up more. "We're going to die on this lonely island. This isn't reality TV, you know."

"Listen," the multimillionaire began. "Five years ago I gave the Republicans $250,000. I gave $500,000 to the Democrats. A year later I increased both amounts by $100,000. Three years ago, since I did extremely well in the stock market, I contributed $750,000 to each Party. Last year business was strong, so I gave a million dollars to both Parties as well as to National Public Radio."

"And the point is?" the chauffeur asked, exasperated.

"It's time for their annual fund drives. I guarantee you—they'll find me."

BLOOPER

Millie Vincent, who lives on West View Court, has lost her pet cat. She said it was last seen near the West View Gun Club and Shooting Range.

Quote

Choose a job you love, and you will never have to work a day in your life.

JOKE

A visiting pastor was preaching a sermon. He got a bit carried away and talked for 2 hours.

Finally he realized what he was doing and said to the congregation, "I'm sorry I talked so long. I left my watch at home."

To which someone replied, "There's a calendar on the far wall."

262

BLOOPER

Gilfords Apparel in Mankato is offering a 10% discount to all Our Savior high school students—but only during school hours.

Quote

Wrinkles should merely indicate where smiles have been.

JOKES

Teacher: Jon, name one important thing we have today that we didn't have 10 years ago.
Jon: Me!

Teacher: I hope I didn't see you looking at Don's paper.
Tim: I hope you didn't either.

BLOOPER

St. Paulina's social society will be celebrating Oktoberfest all September long.

Quote

Youth is that period when the youngster knows everything except how to make a living.

JOKE

A knight and his men returned to their castle after a long, hard day of fighting.

"How are we faring?" asked the king.

"Sire," replied the knight, "I have been pillaging on your behalf all day, completely burning the towns of your enemies to the west."

"What?" shrieked the king. "I don't have any enemies west of here!"

"Oh," said the knight. "Well, you do now."

264

BLOOPER

Abstinence advocate Molly Kelly will speak to area teens on Wednesday. Kelly is the mother of 8 children.

Quote

Some people always have plenty of advice
and plenty of bad examples.

JOKE

There were 2 brothers who were very rich, but also very mean. They played the part of perfect Christians, attending the same church. A week after a fund-raising campaign was kicked off for a new church sanctuary, one of the brothers suddenly died.

The other brother went to see the pastor. Before he could say anything, the brother handed the pastor a check for 5 million dollars earmarked for the new sanctuary.

"You can have the money on one condition," the brother said. "At my brother's funeral, you must say he was a saint." The pastor looked at the check and gave his word.

The next day at the funeral, the pastor said, "Here lies a very mean man. But, compared to his brother, he was a saint."

265
Good Old Ben

A man hailed a cab and as soon as he got in, the cabbie said, "Perfect timing. You're just like Ben."

"Who?"

"Ben Tucker. There's a guy who did everything right. Like being in the right place at the right time. It would have happened like that to Ben."

"There are always a few clouds over everybody," said the rider.

"Not Ben. He was a terrific athlete. He could have gone pro in tennis or golf. He sang like Pavarotti and danced like Fred Astaire."

"He was something, huh?"

"He had a memory like a trap. Never forgot anyone's birthday or anniversary. He knew all about wine and was a gourmet cook whose experiments with recipes were delicious. And talk about a handyman! Ben was a crafts-man who could fix anything. Not like me. I change a fuse, and I black out the whole neighborhood."

"No wonder you remember him."

"Well, I never actually met Ben."

"Then how do you know so much about him?"

"Because I married his widow."

266

BLOOPER

Financial planner Hendon Reeves reminded us all that retirement will be cheaper if we spend less.

Quote

The only way to attain perfection
is to follow the advice you give others.

JOKES

Teacher: In this box, I have a 10-foot snake.
Sam: You can't fool me. Snakes don't have feet.

Teacher: Erin, give me a sentence starting with "I."
Erin: I is . . .
Teacher: No, Erin. Always say, "I am."
Erin: All right. I am the 9th letter of the alphabet.

267

BLOOPER

Come to the Pilgrim Hill church supper tonight and beat the candidates for elder.

Quote

Never start an argument with a person when he's tired—
or when he's well rested.

JOKE

At a large college there was a star athlete who was academically challenged. In one of his classes he sat beside a straight-A student. The professor suspected that the athlete was cheating, but she didn't have actual evidence.

Grading the midterm exam, she saw that for question number 10, the smart student had written, "I don't know the answer."

Immediately checking answer 10 on the athlete's exam, she smiled knowingly. He had written, "Me neither."

268

BLOOPER

According to recent studies, claimed Pastor Ellor, older Christians have an edge in longevity.

Quote

Every argument—except for the one you are in—has two sides.

JOKES

Mother: Why on earth did you swallow the money I gave you?
Derek: You said it was money for lunch.

Teacher: If you had one dollar and you asked your father for another, how many dollars would you have?
Chad: One dollar.
Teacher *(sadly)*: You don't know your arithmetic.
Chad *(sadly)*: You don't know my father.

BLOOPER

The city is offering a free seminar with Jean Murphy of our congregation. She will talk about dog training at the Canine Training Center. No dogs allowed.

Quote

Living involves tearing up one rough draft after another.

JOKE

A veterinarian was feeling ill and went to see her doctor. The doctor asked her all the usual questions about symptoms—when they started, how long had they been occurring, and so on. The vet interrupted him.

"Doc, I don't need to ask my patients these kinds of questions. I can tell what's wrong just by looking at them. Why can't you?"

The doctor looked her up and down, and quickly wrote out a prescription. Handing it to her, he said, "There you are. Of course, if that doesn't work, we'll have to put you to sleep."

270

Part 3

Irritations for a Sane Person

* You rub on hand cream and can't turn the bathroom doorknob to get out.

* People behind you in your line at the supermarket dash ahead of you to a checkout just opening up.

* Your glasses slide off your nose when you perspire.

* You can't look up the correct spelling of a word in the dictionary because you don't know how to spell it.

* You have to inform 5 different sales people in the same store that you're just browsing.

* You have to search 10 minutes for a salesperson in that same store once you've decided to make a purchase.

* You had that pen in your hand only a second ago, and now you can't find it.

* You reach under the table to pick something off the floor and smash your head on the way up.

271

BLOOPER

The Third Baptist Church of Evansville to rename Potter Auditorium to Potter Auditorium.

Quote

To advance, sometimes we have to turn around.

JOKE

Two gas company servicemen—a supervisor and a young trainee—were checking meters in a neighborhood. Parking their truck at one end of the alley they worked their way to the other end. At the last house, a woman looking out her kitchen window saw them.

Just for fun, after finishing the meter check, the supervisor decided to race his coworker back to the truck. As they came tearing up to the truck, they heard someone huffing and puffing behind them. It was the lady from the last house.

"Is something wrong?" the supervisor asked her.

"When you see two people from the gas company running," gasped the woman, "you'd better run too!"

272

BLOOPER

Headline: 4000th Baby Delivered to Church Couple from Uplands

Quote

As parents, we are daily training our children how to raise their children.

JOKE

The moviegoers were waiting in the darkened theater for the upcoming previews to begin. As the screen lit up with a flashy ad for the concessions, the sound was missing.

The unexpected silence continued for several moments. Then, out of the darkness, an irritated voice in the crowd demanded, "Okay, who's got the remote?"

BLOOPER

Seven of the 9 elders of Carbondale Presbyterian voted unanimously to purchase a church bus.

Quote

Saying yes to a child is like blowing up a balloon.
You have to know when to stop.

JOKE

A shopkeeper was nervous when a brand-new business just like his own opened up next door. The new owners hung a huge sign: Best Deals.

His anxiety grew when another competitor opened up on the other side and announced its arrival with an even larger sign: Lowest Prices.

Then the shopkeeper got an idea. He put the biggest sign of all over his own shop. It read: Main Entrance.

274

BLOOPER

The popular Dunk Tank at Elmhurst's Fall Festival will be sponsored by Waste Management.

Quote

Many a person has convictions for which he wants someone else to supply the courage.

JOKE

Little Brandon Smith had just been put to bed for the 22nd time, and his mother's patience was wearing thin. "If I hear you call 'Mom' one more time, you'll be punished," she warned him sternly.

For a while it was quiet, and then a small voice called from the top of the stairs, "Mrs. Smith? Can I please have a drink of water?"

275

Limp Duck

A woman brought a limp duck to a veterinarian. The vet listened for a heartbeat, then shook his head sadly. "I'm so sorry. Your pet has passed away."

"No," the owner wailed. "Shouldn't you do some tests to make sure he's dead? He might just be in a coma."

The vet left the room and returned with a Labrador retriever. The dog put his front paws on the exam table, and sniffed the duck from top to bottom. Looking at the vet with sad eyes, he shook his head.

The vet took the dog out and returned with a cat. The cat jumped up on the table and also sniffed the duck from beak to tail. The cat meowed softly, shook its head, then left the room.

"I'm sorry," the vet said again, "but this is definitely a dead duck." The vet turned to his computer terminal, hit a few keys, and printed out a bill. "You can pay this at the front desk," he said.

The woman couldn't believe her eyes. "You're charging me $500 just to tell me my duck is dead?!"

"If you'd taken my word for it, I wouldn't have charged anything. But what with the Lab report and the Cat scan, the price went up."

276

BLOOPER

Pastor Dunkel said the reason for more bear sightings in West Ridge Park is that there are more bears.

Quote

Willpower is the ability to eat just one salted peanut.

JOKE

Matt's English teacher was a perfectionist and demanded the very best of his students. So the teacher's reaction wasn't surprising when Matt handed in a poor paper.

"This is the worst essay I've ever read," ranted the teacher. "There are so many mistakes that I stopped counting them. I can't understand how one person could have made all of them."

"One person didn't," said Matt defensively. "My father helped me."

BLOOPER

Encourage your child to participate in the Bible drill: The top 50 participants will win a special one-of-a-kind prize.

Quote

Today's tall oak tree is
yesterday's nut that held its ground.

JOKE

During her training as a medical-group receptionist, a young woman was instructed never to recommend one of the clinic's doctors over another. Instead, she was simply to say who had available appointments.

One day a woman came in and leaned over the receptionist's desk. "I'm a nurse," she whispered, "and I know the staff always knows which doctors are good and which aren't. Who do you think I should see?"

Knowing her supervisor was nearby, the receptionist replied sweetly, "I'm sorry. I can't recommend any of our doctors."

"Thanks for the tip!" the woman said, heading out the door.

278

BLOOPER

On a church bulletin board: "Tired of working for only $9.75 an hour? At Mikker Employment we offer profit-sharing and flexible hours. Starting pay $7 to $9 per hour."

Quote

Never let your studies interfere with your education.

JOKE

A newscaster interrupted the regularly scheduled program to announce the outcome of a statewide election.

"More on candidates at 10 p.m.," he said.

A young girl watching TV with her father looked at him in disbelief. "I didn't know they could call politicians 'morons' on television!"

BLOOPER

The Bible is clear: Flee from sexual immortality.

Quote

Do not merely entertain ideas—put them to work.

JOKE

In the exam room, a patient was waiting nervously for a renowned medical specialist.

"So who did you see before coming to me?" asked the doctor.

"My family practitioner."

"Your GP? What a waste of time," the doctor said incredulously. "What useless advice did he give you?"

"He told me to come and see you."

280
Real Political Bloopers

✳ "Things are more like they are now than they have ever been." *President Gerald Ford*

✳ "My fellow astronauts . . ." *Vice-President Dan Quayle,* speaking at an Apollo 11 anniversary celebration.

✳ "Capital punishment is our society's recognition of the sanctity of human life." *Orrin Hatch, senator from Utah,* explaining his support of the death penalty.

✳ "China is a big country, inhabited by many Chinese." *Charles de Gaulle, former French president*

✳ "This is the best disaster in California since I was elected." *California governor Pat Brown,* surveying damage from a devastating flood.

✳ "Gerald Ford was a Communist." *Ronald Reagan* in a speech. He later said he meant to say "Congressman."

✳ "Outside of the killings, Washington, D.C., has one of the lowest crime rates in the country." *Mayor Marion Barry, Washington, D.C.*

✳ "We found the term *killing* too broad." *State Department spokesperson* on why the word *killing* was replaced with "unlawful or arbitrary deprivation of life" in its human rights reports for 1984.

281

BLOOPER

Pastor Bendell claims that rain would end the drought in Servas County.

Quote

Homework is something teenagers do
between phone calls.

JOKE

It was the first day of school for the 1st-grader. After everyone was settled in their seats, the teacher asked the class to stand, put their right hand over their heart, and recite the Pledge of Allegiance.

Scanning the room as the recitation began, the teacher noticed one boy with his hand on the right side of his bottom.

"Johnny, please put your hand over your heart."

"It is over my heart."

"What makes you think that's your heart?" the teacher asked.

"Because every time my grandma comes to visit, she picks me up, pats me here, and says, 'Bless your little heart.'"

282

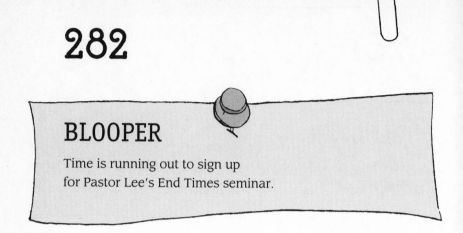

BLOOPER

Time is running out to sign up
for Pastor Lee's End Times seminar.

Quote

Never read the fine print.
There is no way you're going to like it.

JOKE

A woman took pride in her homemade freezer meals
which she labeled clearly: Meatloaf, Pot Roast, Pork and
Vegetables, Chicken and Dumplings, or Beef Pot Pie.

Whenever she asked her husband what he wanted for
dinner, he never requested any of those choices. So she
decided to relabel the entrees according to his requests.

Open the freezer now and you'll see: Whatever,
Anything, I Don't Know, I Don't Care, Something Good,
or Food.

BLOOPER

The menu at the retreat for deaconesses featured a tasty meat sauce over pastor.

Quote

There is no free tuition in the school of hard knocks.

JOKE

A man and a little boy entered a barbershop together. After the man received the full treatment—shave, manicure, and haircut—he boosted the boy into the chair.

"I need to pick something up," he said. "I'll be back in a few minutes."

When the boy's haircut was done, the man still hadn't returned. "It looks like your daddy forgot about you," the barber said.

"That wasn't my daddy," said the boy. "He just walked in here when I did and said, 'Come on, son, we're going to get a free haircut!'"

284

Quote

The right temperature at home is maintained by
warm hearts—not hot heads.

JOKE

Shopping for a flannel nightgown at the mall, an older
woman stopped in at a store known for its sexy lingerie.

To her delight, she found just what she was looking for.
Waiting to pay, she noticed a young woman behind her
holding the same nightgown.

I'm not over the hill yet, she thought. *I still know fashion
when I see it.*

Turning to the 20-something woman behind her, she
said, "I see we have the same taste."

"Oh, I'm glad you like the gown," the younger woman
replied. "Now I'm certain my grandmother will love it!"

285

Only in America . . .

* can a pizza get to your house faster than an ambulance;
* are there handicap parking places in front of a skating rink;
* do people order double cheeseburgers, large fries, and a diet soda;
* do banks leave both doors open and then chain the pens to the counters;
* do we leave cars worth thousands of dollars in the driveway and leave useless junk in boxes in the garage;
* do we use answering machines to screen calls and then have call waiting so we won't miss a call from someone we didn't want to talk to in the first place;
* do we buy hot dogs in packages of 10 and buns in packages of 8;
* do we use the word *politics* to accurately describe the process: *Poli* in Latin means "many" and *tics* are "blood-sucking creatures."

286

BLOOPER

An arsonist destroyed the Luther League's annual bonfire.

Quote

Before borrowing money from a friend,
it's good to decide which you need the most.

JOKE

A new counselor had been assigned to lead a support group for visually-impaired adults. Many of the participants had macular degeneration, which made it difficult for them to distinguish facial features.

At the first meeting, the counselor introduced himself. Knowing that many in the group would not be able to see him well, he jokingly said, "For those of you who can't see how I look, I've been told that I am a cross between Paul Newman and Robert Redford."

Immediately, one woman called out, "We're not *that* blind!"

287

BLOOPER

The weekly Tuesday morning ladies Bible study meets on the second Thursday of every month in the Fireside room.

Quote

A true friend will remember your birthday but forget how many you've had.

JOKE

Steve found a ransom note under his front door. "Bring $50,000 to the 17th hole of your country club by 11:00 a.m. if you ever want to see your wife alive again." By the time Steve got to the designated spot, it was well past 2 p.m.

A masked man stepped out from behind a bush and demanded, "You're 3 hours late. What took you so long?"

"Give me a break!" said Steve, waving his scorecard. "I have a 27 handicap."

BLOOPER

Pastor Williams thanked all the hunters for participating in the "Blessing of the Hunt." The annual deer hunt got off to a safe start with only 1 death and 9 accidents.

Quote

Be grateful for doors of opportunity—
and for friends who keep the hinges oiled.

JOKE

Two bowling teams, one made up of all blondes and one comprised of all brunettes, chartered a double-decker bus for a weekend tournament in Atlantic City.

On their first ride, the brunettes rode inside the bus and the blondes rode outside on the upper deck. The brunettes were loudly whooping it up when their team captain realized it was awfully quiet upstairs. She decided to go up and investigate.

When the brunette captain stepped out on the upper deck, she found all the blondes clutching their seats in sheer terror. "What is going on up here?" the brunette asked. "We're having a great time downstairs!"

To which the blonde team captain replied, "Yeah, but you've got a driver!"

289

BLOOPER

Blue Ridge Septic Services will sponsor the church's candy booth at the Fall Festival.

Quote

The smart husband never asks who is boss around the house.

JOKE

A mother received a phone message from her son's school to pick him up at the principal's office.

When the mother arrived, the principal was startled to see her wearing pajamas and with curlers in her hair. "Why are you dressed like that?" the principal asked.

"I told my son that if he ever did anything to embarrass me, I would embarrass him back," she said. "So I've come to spend the day with him."

Part 1
Dog Dictionary

* Dog bed: Any soft, clean surface, such as the white bedspread in the guest room or the newly upholstered couch in the living room.

* Drool: What you do when your human has food and you don't. To do this properly, you must sit as close as you can, look sad, and let the drool fall on their shoes, or better yet, on their lap.

* Garbage can: An aromatic container that your neighbors put out once a week to test your ingenuity. Stand on your hind legs and push the lid off. If you do it right, you are rewarded with paper to shred, bones to consume, and stale pieces of bread to scatter throughout the neighborhood.

* Leash: A strap that attaches to your collar, enabling you to lead your human everywhere you want him or her to go.

* Sniff: A social custom to use when you greet other dogs. Place your nose as close as you can to the other dog's rear end and inhale deeply; repeat several times, or until your human makes you stop.

BLOOPER

During the last service project, the senior students in the Route 45 youth group cooked and served grandparents.

Quote

The best way to remember your wife's birthday is to forget it once.

JOKE

A man phoned an airline to find out departure and arrival times for a flight from Indianapolis to Chicago. Unaware that Indianapolis is on eastern standard time and Chicago is on central standard time, he was quite surprised when the ticket agent said, "The next flight leaves at 1:00 p.m., and arrives in Chicago at 1:10 p.m."

"What did you say?" the man asked.

The agent repeated the times, then said, "Do you want a reservation?"

"No, thanks," the man replied. "But I think I'll come to the airport to watch that thing take off!"

292

BLOOPER

Clyde Almers of the Valley View School District sent this announcement: I am putting a church team together for the Prairie County Spelling Be. Pleas call me if interested.

Quote

More tools are ruined by rust than by overuse.

JOKE

Two wildlife documentary filmmakers were filming lions in Africa. They both noticed a particularly aggressive lion getting ready to attack them. Putting down his camera, one filmmaker slowly changed from his boots into a pair of running shoes. The other man said, "You know you can't outrun a lion, don't you?"

"The way I see it," the first filmmaker said, "all I have to do is keep ahead of you, and I'll be all right!"

BLOOPER

The church board of elders has called a special meeting today to decide what it did last week.

Quote

The problem with ignorance—
it picks up confidence as it goes along.

JOKE

A young city slicker wanted to be a cowboy more than anything else. One summer, a rancher decided to give him a chance.

"This is a lariat," the rancher said, handing the cowboy wannabe a rope on his first day. "We use it to catch cows."

"I see," said the young man, examining it carefully. "What do you use for bait?"

294

BLOOPER

Students are selling discount books for up to 150% off your favorite restaurant meal.

Quote

If you skate on thin ice, you end up in hot water.

JOKE

One day a young mother was sick in bed at home. Even though her daughter was only 4 years old, she always tried to "help" mommy. She got some magazines for her mom, fluffed all the pillows, and even made her a cup of hot tea.

Delighted with the care, her mother asked, "Who taught you how to make tea?"

"Oh, Mommy, I've seen you do it lots of times," the youngster said. "But I couldn't find the strainer, so I used the fly swatter instead."

"You what?" her mother said in alarm.

"Don't worry, Mommy. I didn't use the new fly swatter—I used the old one."

295

Part 2
Dog Dictionary

* **Bicycles:** Two-wheeled exercise machines, invented for dogs to control body fat. To get maximum aerobic benefit, hide behind a bush. When you spot one, dash out, bark loudly, and run alongside for a few yards. The human on the bike will swerve and fall into the bushes.

* **Deafness:** This malady kicks in when your human calls. Symptoms include either running in the opposite direction or simply lying down.

* **Thunder:** This is a signal that the world is coming to an end. Humans remain amazingly calm during thunderstorms, so it is necessary to warn them of the danger by trembling uncontrollably, panting, rolling your eyes wildly, whimpering or barking incessantly, and never letting them out of your sight.

* **Wastebasket:** This is a doggie treasure chest regularly stocked with a changing array of interesting things. When you get bored, turn the basket over and strew the contents all over the house. When your human comes home, they're sure to express their excitement with your creative decorating.

296

Quote

Even if you own a 15-bedroom house,
you can only sleep in one room at a time.

JOKE

A woman heard an unexpected knock at her front door. Looking through the peephole she asked, "Who's there?"

"Parcel post, ma'am. I have a package that needs a signature."

"Where's the package?" the woman asked suspiciously. The deliveryman held it up.

"Could I see some ID?" she said, still not convinced.

"Lady, if I wanted to break into your house, I'd probably just use these," he said wearily, holding up the set of keys she had left in the door.

BLOOPER

Marvin Bitts said if anyone in church likes to eat squirrels, he'll shoot them. Call him in the evenings.

Quote

When a man is poor, the doctor tells him he has an itch— if he's rich, he has an allergy.

JOKE

A man who hated his wife's cat decided to get rid of it. He drove 20 blocks from home and let the cat go. But when he returned home, the cat was sitting in the driveway.

The next day the man decided to drop the cat 40 blocks away, but the exact same thing happened again.

The 3rd day he drove 10 miles away, turned left, went past a bridge, made 2 rights, 3 lefts, crossed some railroad tracks, and made another right before he stopped and scooted the cat out of the car.

Hours later, the man called his wife. "Jen, do you see the cat?"

"Yes. Why?"

"Put that cat on the phone," he said in frustration. "I need directions back home."

298

Quote

If playing the piano by ear, be careful not to get your earring caught in the keys.

JOKE

One day a housework-challenged husband decided to wash a new sweatshirt.

A moment after he stepped into the laundry room, he shouted to his wife, "What setting do I use on the washing machine?"

"It depends," she replied. "What does it say on your shirt?"

"University of Auburn."

BLOOPER

We will be featuring old-time chili fixings at our chili supper tonight. The fixings are made from the original cook, Lucille Hethers.

Quote

You should not stop laughing as you grow old—
but you'll grow old if you stop laughing.

JOKE

An elderly gent was invited to dinner at the home of an old friend. Throughout the conversation, the guest was impressed by the way his friend preceded every request to his wife with endearing terms—Honey, My Love, Darling, Sweetheart, Pumpkin, etc. The couple had been married almost 70 years and, clearly, they were still very much in love.

While the wife was in the kitchen, the guest leaned over and said to his host, "I think it's wonderful that, after all these years, you still call your wife loving nicknames."

To which the husband replied with a sheepish smile, "The truth is, I forgot her name about 10 years ago."

300
Warning: Hormones

There are times when a woman can be a little moody. Every man should refer to this handy conversation guide if he knows what's good for him.

Dangerous: What's for dinner?
Safer: Can I help you with dinner?
Safest: Where would you like to go for dinner?

Dangerous: Are you wearing that?!?
Safer: Brown is a good color on you.
Safest: Wow! Look at you!

Dangerous: Should you be eating that dessert?
Safer: You know, there's a lot of cake left.
Safest: Can I get you another piece?

Dangerous: What did you do all day?
Safer: I hope you didn't overdo it today.
Safest: Anything more that needs to be done?

BLOOPER

Church newsletter classifieds: For sale—1992 Catholic Deville. Clean. $3,000.

Quote

Parents never fully appreciate teachers until it rains all day.

JOKE

A man is driving down a road. A woman is driving down the same road from the opposite direction. As they pass each other, the woman leans out the window and yells, "Pig!"

The man immediately leans out his window and yells, "Stupid!"

They each continue on their way. When the man rounds the next curve, he crashes into a huge pig in the middle of the road and just misses getting killed.

Thought for the Day: If men would only listen.

302

BLOOPER

During the seminar there will be a panel discussion of the pros and cons of religious bigotry.

Quote

Don't do anything at home that you don't want your children to do in public.

JOKE

A salesman is driving down a country road when he sees a young kid in front of a barn. On the barn are painted 5 targets with arrows in the bull's-eye of each target. Screeching to a halt, he runs over to the kid.

"Son," he says, "how did you hit all those bull's-eyes?"

"Well, I took each arrow, licked my fingers, and straightened the feathers like this," the boy demonstrated. "Then I aimed with my hand against my cheek, let go, and wherever the arrow landed, I drew a bull's-eye."

BLOOPER

Church newsletter classifieds: Elsa Burket has a dog to be given away to a good home. Part German shepherd mix. Possibly female. Could also be male.

Quote

Only a mediocre person is always at his best.

JOKE

In California's Sonoma Valley, where vineyards cater to wine snobbery, a woman phoned the classified ad department of a newspaper. She had what sounded like "well-aged Caumeneur" for sale.

The ad rep was unfamiliar with that particular wine but was used to the infusion of French words into the local vocabulary.

"Could you please spell that?" she asked.

"You know," said the woman impatiently, "C-o-w-m-a-n-u-r-e."

BLOOPER

Herman Wilson has asked the congregation to keep an eye open for one of his Black Angus steers. The animal was last seen near Wallace Brothers BBQ on Route 42.

Quote

Most people use very weak thread when mending their ways.

JOKE

The 4th-grade teacher had to leave the room for a few minutes. When she returned, she was surprised to find all of her students sitting quietly.

"I've never seen anything like it before," the teacher said. "This is wonderful. But why are you being so well-behaved?"

Finally, one girl spoke up. "Yesterday you said that if you ever came back and found us quiet, you would drop dead."

305

Ghost Car

In the middle of a snowstorm on a very dark night, a man was trying to hitch a ride with no luck. The snow was so blinding, he could barely see his hand in front of him. Suddenly, car lights appeared behind him. It stopped!

The guy immediately got in the backseat of the car before realizing that nobody was behind the wheel.

The car started slowly. The guy looked at the road and saw a treacherous curve ahead. He started praying loudly. Just in time, a hand appeared through the driver's window and turned the steering wheel. This happened over and over again.

Finally, he had seen enough. The guy jumped out of the car, and ran to the nearest town. Cold, covered with snow, and in shock, he ran into a tavern and downed two shots of whiskey before recounting his horrible ordeal.

About half an hour later, two other guys walked into the same tavern, cold and covered with snow. Pointing to the man at the counter, one said to the other, "Look! That's the crazy guy who climbed into the car while we were pushing it into town!"

306

BLOOPER

Dr. Ross told the women's group that carpet tunnel syndrome is often misdiagnosed and misunderstood.

Quote

Stand up to be seen, speak up to be heard, and shut up to be appreciated.

JOKE

A woman was sitting in the exam room, waiting for her new doctor to read through her extensive medical history.

Looking through all 17 pages, the doctor said, "You look better in person than you do on paper."

BLOOPER

The Wilson Street Baptist Church board of deacons announced their new health policy to the staff. They said that getting sick now requires a written 2-day notice.

Quote

There are very few short sermons that are bad.

JOKE

A 1st-grader, who had worn glasses since the age of 3, came home from school at the end of the first week very distressed. "Honey, what happened today to upset you so much?" his mother asked.

"It's not fair that I'm not allowed to go to the library."

"Why aren't you allowed to go to the library?"

"Because," he said on the verge of tears, "in order to go to the library you have to have super-vision, and I wear glasses!"

BLOOPER

The St. Christopher bipolar group has planned
2 meetings this month.

Quote

Even liars are a whole lot easier to believe
when they are saying nice things about us.

JOKE

Two boys were picking walnuts from a tree near a
cemetery fence. When their bucket was full, they stopped
to divide up the bounty.

Just then another boy on a bike rode past the cemetery
and heard, "One for you, one for me."

"It's Satan and the Lord dividing up souls at the cemetery," he shuddered.

Pedaling as fast as he could, he nearly ran over an old
man with a cane. "Quick," said the boy. "Satan and the
Lord are at the cemetery dividing up souls."

Sure enough, the old man heard it too: "One for you,
one for me." Then he and the boy heard more terrifying
words: "Let's get those nuts by the fence." Folks say the
old guy made it back to town 5 minutes before the boy.

BLOOPER

All absentee ballots for the election of elders must be presented in person.

Quote

Help a man out of trouble and you can be sure of one thing—he won't forget you the next time he's in trouble.

JOKE

Farmer Jones's cows recently stopped giving good milk. So Farmer Jones asked other farmers for advice. When someone told him that happy cows give good milk, Farmer Jones began telling jokes to his cows every morning. They would all laugh. The neighboring cows thought that the jokes were pretty stupid. Because of this, Farmer Jones's cows became the laughingstock of the town.

310
Ice Fishing

On a cold winter day, an old man walked out onto a frozen lake, cut a hole in the ice, dropped in his fishing line, and waited. An hour passed without even a nibble. Then a young boy walked out onto the ice, cut a hole in the ice 3 feet away, and dropped in his fishing line. A minute later, *bam!* A largemouth bass hit his hook, and the boy pulled in an 18-pounder.

The old man couldn't believe it. He figured it was just luck. But the boy dropped in his line and again within just a few minutes, *bam!* another bass. This went on until finally the old man, who hadn't caught a thing, couldn't take it anymore.

"Son, I've been here for over an hour without even a nibble. You've been here only 15 minutes and have caught about half a dozen fish! What's your secret?"

"Roo raf roo reep ra rums rarrm," the boy replied.

"What was that?" the old man asked.

"Roo raf roo reep ra rums rarrm."

"Look," said the old man. "I can't understand a word you're saying."

The boy spit into his hand and said, "You have to keep the worms warm!"

BLOOPER

The anger management seminar at St. Vincent's was marred as a brawl erupted, forcing officials to cancel the rest of the event.

Quote

Everyone loves a speaker who says,
"To make a long story short . . ." and then does.

JOKE

A man in Phoenix called his son in New York and said, "Your mother and I are divorcing—35 years is enough. I'm sick of talking about this, so you call your sister in Chicago and tell her." Then he hung up.

Frantic, the son called his sister. "A divorce? I don't think so!" she said angrily. "I'll take care of this."

She called her father immediately and yelled, "You are not getting divorced! Don't do a single thing until we get there. Do you hear me?" And she hung up.

The father turned to his wife. "Okay," he said. "It worked. They're coming for Thanksgiving and paying their own way. Now we have to think up something for Christmas!"

312

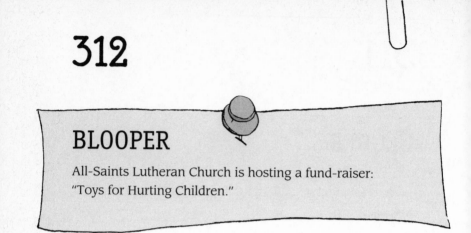

BLOOPER

All-Saints Lutheran Church is hosting a fund-raiser: "Toys for Hurting Children."

Quote

When a mule has it, no one calls it willpower.

JOKE

A famous treasure hunter went out one day with all of his diving gear to search for a treasure chest that was supposed to be on a sunken ship. He swam around for a while and looked where the treasure was supposed to be, but he didn't find anything. Walking toward shore in the shallow water, he tripped on something. He started to dig around, when voilà—it was the treasure chest he had been looking for!

All this goes to prove that booty is only shin deep!

BLOOPER

The Holy Trinity Methodist Church women will discuss "Salary Equity within Women's Ministries" at their luncheon. The cost is $15 for women and $20 for men.

Quote

Time is like a snowflake—it disappears when we are trying to decide what to do with it.

JOKE

"When I was a young," complained the frustrated father, "I was disciplined by being sent to my room without dinner. But our son has his own color TV, phone, computer, and CD player."

"So what do you do when your son misbehaves?" asked his friend.

"I send him to our room!"

314

BLOOPER

Attorney Robert Lewis explained to the Sunday school group that his client was not that guilty.

Quote

There is nothing wrong with the younger generation
that 20 years won't cure.

JOKE

In an upscale pet-supply store, a customer wanted to buy a sweater for her dog. The clerk suggested that she bring her dog in for a proper fit.

"I can't do that!" the lady said. "The sweater is a surprise!"

Part 3
Dog Dictionary

* Bath: This is a process by which humans drench the floor, walls, and themselves with your help. For added fun, shake vigorously and frequently.

* Bump: The best way to get your human's attention when they are drinking a hot cup of coffee or tea.

* Goose Bump: A last-resort maneuver to use when the Bump doesn't get the attention you require.

* Lean: Every good dog's response to the command "Sit," especially if your human is dressed for an evening out. Incredibly effective before black-tie events. Your hair adds a personal touch to the outfit.

* Love: A feeling of intense affection, given freely and without restriction. Show your love by wagging your tail and giving slobbery kisses. If you're lucky, a human will love you in return.

* Sofas: This is your doggie napkin. After eating, it is polite to run up and down the front of the sofa and wipe your face clean.

316

BLOOPER

St. Paul's "A Night of a Thousand Stars" will be held at the Fairview Hilton. Attire is optional.

Quote

Poverty is a state of mind caused by a neighbor's new car.

JOKE

A man was working at home when the doorbell rang. At the door stood a 6-foot-tall cockroach that promptly punched the man between the eyes and ran off.

The next evening, the doorbell rang again. It was the cockroach. Before the man could react, the giant insect spit on him, and kicked him before running away.

The 3rd evening, the cockroach broke into the house and stabbed the man several times, then disappeared. The man crawled to the telephone and called 911. The paramedics rushed him to the hospital in time.

The next morning the man was reounting to his doctor what had happened. "Yes," the doctor nodded, "there's definitely a nasty bug going around."

BLOOPER

Citizen's alert:
Do your child have an education funding plan?

Quote

One thing about ignorance—it can cause a lot of interesting arguments.

JOKES

Q: Did you hear about the guy who lost his left arm and leg in a car crash?
A: He's all right now.

Q: What do Eskimos get from sitting on the ice too long?
A: Polaroids.

Q: What do prisoners use to call each other?
A: Cell phones.

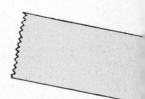

318

BLOOPER

Stan Austin, of Austin Brother Memorials, says that it's best to avoid the Christmas rush and shop early for your cemetery needs.

Quote

When man figured out that he could not live by bread alone, he invented the sandwich.

JOKE

It was the pregame pep talk. "Remember," the coach challenged his team in the locker room, "the game is all about individual skills, initiative, and leadership. Now go out there and do exactly what I tell you."

BLOOPER

Open house at Christie Spark's Exercise World.
There will be free coffee and donuts.

Quote

The self-made man all too often admires his maker.

JOKE

A woman was down to her last $50 at the roulette tables
in Vegas. Exasperated, she exclaimed, "I've had such
rotten luck today! What in the world should I do now?"

A man next to her suggested, "Why don't you play your
age?" Then he walked away.

Moments later, the man heard a commotion at the
roulette table. He rushed back, pushing his way through
the crowd. The woman was on the floor, with the
roulette operator kneeling over her. "What happened? Is
she all right?" the man asked.

"I don't know," the operator replied. "She put all her
money on 29, and 36 came up. Then she fainted!"

320
Cat Quotes

* Cats are smarter than dogs. You can't get 8 cats to pull a sled through snow.

* From a cat's perspective, all things belong to cats.

* One cat just leads to another.

* Dogs come when they're called; cats take a message and get back to you later.

* Cats are delicate creatures subject to a good many ailments, but none of them suffer from insomnia.

* People who hate cats will come back as mice in their next life.

* There are many intelligent species in the universe. They are all owned by cats.

* Dogs believe they are human. Cats believe they are God.

* Cats base their actions on the principle that it never does any harm to ask for what you want.

* Cats aren't clean; they're just covered with cat spit.

BLOOPER

The 3 wise men brought gifts of golf, frankincense, and myrrh.

Quote

A steering committee is 4 people trying to park a car.

JOKE

Dear Dad,
$chool i$ really great. I am making lot$ of friend$ and $tudying very hard.
   With all my $tuff, I $imply can't think of anything I need. $o if you would like, you can ju$t $end me a card, becau$e I would love to hear from you.
Your $on

Dear Son,
I kNOw that astroNOmy, ecoNOmics, and oceaNOgraphy are eNOugh to keep even an hoNOr student busy. Do NOt forget that the pursuit of kNOwledge is a NOble task, and NOthing should distract you from reaching your goal.
Dad

322

BLOOPER

Due to unforeseen complications, the debate between Pastor Lucas and the town's only psychic, Miss Clare, had to be postponed until a later date.

Quote

An egotist is a self-made man who insists on giving everyone else the recipe.

JOKE

A woman found an ornate bottle on the beach, rubbed it, and a genie appeared. The genie said, "I'm a one-wish genie. So what'll it be?"

The woman said, "See this map of the Middle East? I want all of the people in these countries to love each other."

"These countries have been at war for years! I'm good," said the genie, "but not that good! Make another wish."

The woman said, "Well, I've never been able to find the right man. One who's considerate and fun, likes to cook and help clean, gets along with my family, isn't glued to the TV, and is faithful. That's my wish."

The genie held out his hand. "Let me take a look at that map again."

323

BLOOPER

In lieu of flowers for Bob Hauser, donations can be sent to his daughter-in-law, Jean Armstrong, so she can buy the big-screen television that the widow wants.

Quote

The best substitute for experience is being 16.

JOKES

Ratio of igloo's circumference to its diameter:
Eskimo Pi

Two thousand pounds of Chinese soup: Won ton

One millionth of a mouthwash: One microscope

324

BLOOPER

The pastor took an informal poll of the congregation and found that 60 percent preferred man-made Christmas trees, while the rest preferred artificial trees.

Quote

Never let a fool kiss you—and never let a kiss fool you.

JOKE

Some great truths from a child's point of view:

When your mom is mad at your dad, don't let her brush your hair.

If your sister hits you, don't hit her back. Parents always catch the 2nd person.

Never ask your 3-year-old brother to hold a tomato.

You can't hide a piece of broccoli in a glass of milk.

325

Part 1

Hmmm . . .

* Why could Superman stop bullets with his chest but always ducked when someone threw a gun at him?

* How would you design a chair if your knees bent the other way?

* If *con* is the opposite of *pro,* what is the opposite of progress?

* Why does lemon juice have mostly artificial ingredients, but dishwashing liquid contains real lemons?

* How much deeper would the ocean be if sponges didn't grow in it?

* Why do we wash bath towels? Aren't we clean when we use them?

* Why do we put suits in a garment bag and put garments in a suitcase?

* Why doesn't glue stick to the inside of the bottle?

* Do Roman paramedics refer to IV's as "4's"?

* Whose idea was it for the word *lisp* to have an *s* in it?

* What do little birdies see when they get knocked unconscious?

326

BLOOPER

Faith Banning is looking for any lady in the congregation who has a cake pan to swap. She has a 9-inch by 13-inch pan and would like a 13-inch by 9-inch pan.

Quote

Advice is like cooking—
you should try it before you feed it to others.

JOKES

Why is the alphabet in that order? Is it because of that song?

If the black box flight recorder is never damaged during a plane crash, why isn't the whole airplane made out of the same stuff?

Why is there an expiration date on sour cream?

If most car accidents occur within five miles of home, why doesn't everyone just move ten miles away?

BLOOPER

Cash is the key to ending church financial problems, claimed financial advisor Ralph Wittser.

Quote

Sometimes what looks like a light at the end of the tunnel is an oncoming train.

JOKE

Odd signs:

In a laundromat: Automatic washing machines. Please remove all your clothes when the light goes out.

In a London department store: Bargain Basement Upstairs.

In an office: Would the person who took the step ladder yesterday please bring it back? Otherwise further steps will be taken.

328

Quote

It is never wise to argue with a fool—bystanders won't be able to see the difference between the two of you.

JOKES

Time between slipping on a peel and smacking the pavement: One bananosecond

Weight an evangelist carries with God: One billigram

Time it takes to sail 220 yards at one nautical mile per hour: Knot-furlong

BLOOPER

The deaf ministry at the Gordon Street Bible Church
is holding a silent auction next Saturday.

Quote

There is nothing friendlier in the world than a wet dog.

JOKES

In my day, we couldn't afford shoes, so we went barefoot.
In the winter we had to wrap our feet with barbed wire for
traction.

In my day, we didn't have time for fun. There was only
time for work, time to eat, and time for sleep. The sheriff
would go around and tell everyone when to change.

330

Full Service Shopping

Jacob, 85, and Rebecca, 79, were excited about their upcoming wedding. Out for a stroll, they stopped at a drugstore.

Jacob said to the pharmacist. "Do you sell heart medication?"

Pharmacist: "Of course we do."

Jacob: "How about medicine for circulation?"

Pharmacist: "All kinds."

Jacob: "Medicine for rheumatism?"

Pharmacist: "Definitely."

Jacob: "Medicine for memory?"

Pharmacist: "Yes, a large variety."

Jacob: "What about vitamins and sleeping pills?"

Pharmacist: "Absolutely."

Jacob: "You have loose bowel and gas pills?"

Pharmacist: "Yes, with plenty of generics."

Jacob: "What about paraphernalia for diabetes?"

Pharmacist: "Of course. You name any condition, and we have what you need."

Jacob: "Perfect! We'd like to register here for our wedding gifts."

BLOOPER

Fourth Baptist is hosting a fund-raising dinner for the Larimars due to Ralph's recent heart attack. The menu features chicken-fried steak, fries, brats, and deep-dish pecan pie.

Quote

What the world needs is more geniuses with humility because there are so few of us left.

JOKES

More odd signs:

In a British office: After the tea break, staff should empty the teapot and stand upside down on the draining board.

On a church door: This is the gate to heaven. Enter ye all by this door. (This door is kept locked because of the draft. Please use side entrance.)

Outside a secondhand shop: We exchange anything—bicycles, washing machines, etc. Why not bring your wife and get a wonderful bargain?

332

BLOOPER

Bethel Chapel's Pastor McWilliams reminded the congregation, "We put the *M* in religion."

Quote

You've never heard of a woman making a fool out of a man without a lot of cooperation.

JOKE

Planning a Thanksgiving weekend of entertaining guests, I was making a list of things I needed to do, including taking food out of the freezer and grocery shopping.

Just then, a friend whom I had been promising to take to lunch called and asked if we could make it that day.

Knowing that I would be shopping after lunch, I taped my "to do" list to the car dashboard before I picked my friend up.

A moment after she got in the car, she said indignantly, "Thanks a lot!"

I quickly put two and two together. She had read the first item on my list: "Take out the turkey."

BLOOPER

The counseling seminar at St. Peter's is for men and women only.

Quote

A racehorse is an amazing animal—
it can take several thousand people for
a ride at the same time.

JOKES

Half of a large intestine: One semicolon.

One thousand pains: One kiloahurtz.

Basic unit of laryngitis: One hoarsepower.

Shortest distance between 2 jokes: A straight line.

334

Quote

Some people soak up ideas like a blotter—
except they get it all backwards.

JOKE

After a long career in teaching, certain changes signal you are about to retire:

Fellow staff members greet you in the hall with, "Oh, stop smiling!"

You get up to the checkout counter at Borders, and you realize you're buying books you won't need next year.

Your file cabinets are getting lighter, and your circular file is getting heavier.

You get in line at the copy machine and realize you don't have anything to copy.

335

Signs You Went Nuts on Thanksgiving

* The gravy boat your wife set out was a 12-footer!
* Your after-dinner moans were loud enough that an ambulance radio intercepted them.
* Paramedics had to bring in the Jaws of Life to pry you out of the EZ-Boy.
* Your "Big Elvis Super-Belt" won't go around your waist anymore.
* You set off 3 earthquake seismographs on your Friday morning jog.
* You receive a Sumo wrestler application via e-mail.
* Pricking your finger for cholesterol screening produced a glob of gravy.
* That rash on your stomach is steering-wheel burn.
* Representatives from the Butterball Hall of Fame call twice.
* You consider gluttony as your patriotic duty.

336

Quote

I misplaced our Christmas card list. Now I don't know
who our friends are.

JOKES

If some people think that man evolved from monkeys and
apes, how do they explain why we still have monkeys
and apes?

I went to a bookstore and asked the saleswoman,
"Where's the self-help section?" She said if she told me,
it would defeat the purpose.

If all those psychics know the winning lottery numbers,
why are they all still working?

BLOOPER

Remember—when sending your Christmas packages to our missionaries, please use partial post.

Quote

An inventor is a crackpot who becomes a genius when his idea catches on.

JOKE

Martha Stewart's way: Stuff a miniature marshmallow in the bottom of a sugar cone to prevent ice cream drips.

The real woman's way: Bite a hole in the bottom of the cone and just suck the ice cream right out.

338

BLOOPER

The Taylor Bible Chapel is selling fresh-cut Christmas trees. The trees will arrive December 28.

Quote

Never put off until tomorrow what you can do today.If you wait until tomorrow, they will either have taxed it or made it illegal.

JOKE

A woman went to the post office to buy stamps for her Christmas cards.

"What denomination?" asked the clerk.

"Oh, good heavens! Have we come to this?" said the woman. "Then, give me 50 Baptist stamps and 50 Catholic ones."

BLOOPER

Sign in a church: If we see smoking, we will assume you are on fire and take appropriate action.

Quote

The cards are badly shuffled—until I get a good hand.

JOKE

It was the beginning of winter and the radio announcer gave listeners this reminder: "We're expecting 3 to 4 inches of snow today. Park on the even-numbered side of the street so the snowplow can get through." Dutifully, one woman went out and moved her car.

A week later, the announcer said, "We're expecting 4 to 5 inches of snow today. Park on the odd-numbered side of the street." The same woman moved her car again.

The next week the announcer began, "We are expecting a real blizzard today. You must park—" then *phhhttttt* the power went out.

The woman panicked, not knowing what to do, until her husband calmly said, "Why don't you leave the car in the garage this time?"

340

English Is an Odd Language . . .

There is no egg in the eggplant,
No ham in the hamburger,
And neither pine nor apple in the pineapple.
English muffins were not invented in England.
French fries were not invented in France.

If writers write, how come fingers don't fing.
If the plural of tooth is teeth,
Shouldn't the plural of booth be beeth?
If the teacher taught,
Why didn't the preacher praught?

If a vegetarian eats vegetables,
What does a humanitarian eat?
Why do people recite at a play, yet play at a recital?
Park on driveways and drive on parkways?

English reflects the creativity of the human race,
Which, of course, isn't a race at all.
That is why: When the stars are out they are visible,
But when the lights are out they are invisible.
And why it is that when I wind up my watch, it starts,
But when I wind up this poem, it ends.

BLOOPER

The youth group of Aliquippa Baptist is selling donuts as a fund-raiser. The cost is a dozen donuts for a $1.00—limit 2 donuts per customer, please.

Quote

A visitor to Reno was so unlucky that he
lost his shirt in a coin laundry.

JOKE

A man bought his wife a beautiful diamond ring for Christmas.

"I thought she wanted one of those sporty 4-wheel drive vehicles," his friend remarked.

"She did," he replied. "But where am I going to find a fake Jeep?"

342

Quote

There is no such thing as childproofing your house.

JOKE

A Nativity scene displayed in a small southern town's main square got the attention of a visitor from the North. The traditional crèche had one odd feature—each wise man was wearing a fireman's helmet.

Puzzled, the out-of-towner stopped at a nearby store and asked the clerk about the helmets. "You Yankees never read the Bible, do you?" the clerk chided sweetly.

The man assured the woman that he did, but he simply couldn't recall anything about firemen in the Bible.

Pulling a Bible from behind the counter, the clerk rustled through some pages. Finally she stopped and pointed, saying proudly: "See, it says right here, 'The three wise men came from afar.' "

BLOOPER

Church newsletter classifieds:
Snowblower for sale—outdoor model.

Quote

A 4-year-old's voice is louder than 200 adults
in a crowded restaurant.

JOKE

School was called off due to a heavy snowstorm. When
the children returned a few days later, one teacher asked
her young students whether they had used the time away
from school constructively.

"I sure did," one little girl replied. "I kept praying for
more snow."

344

BLOOPER

Our elders debate next year's budget—
and more lies ahead.

Quote

When you hear the toilet flush and the words "uh-oh,"
it's already too late.

JOKE

Martha Stewart's way: When a cake recipe calls for
flouring the baking pan, use some of the dry cake mix
instead, and there won't be any white residue on the
bottom of the cake.

The real woman's way: Go to the bakery. Buy a cake.
They'll even decorate it for you.

345
You Might Be a Scrooge if . . .

* you turn on the lawn sprinklers on Christmas Eve to keep carolers away;

* you buy all of your Christmas gifts at a convenient mart;

* your favorite version of "The Nutcracker" stars members of *The Sopranos*;

* you get your Christmas tree at a rest stop in the middle of the night;

* your idea of Christmas dinner is a hunk of summer sausage and a cheese log;

* you think "Ho, Ho, Ho" is a line from a Rocky movie;

* your favorite version of "Silent Night" is sung by Homer Simpson;

* your favorite pastime is putting defective bulbs in your neighbors' string of Christmas lights or defacing Christmas lawn inflatables with eggnog;

* your only holiday decoration is a rotting pumpkin.

346

BLOOPER

Church newsletter classifieds:
For sale—very old wood dresses.

Quote

Why does Christmas come when the stores
are so crowded?

JOKE

Wisdom and advice for parents:

Shouting to make your children obey is like using the horn to steer your car—and you get about the same results!

The smartest advice on raising children is to enjoy them while they are still on your side.

Avenge yourself. Live long enough to be a problem to your children.

The best way to keep kids at home is to give it a loving atmosphere. And hide the keys to the car.

BLOOPER

Doctor Larsen told the MOPS audience that healthy patients are easier to care for.

Quote

It may be that your sole purpose in life is simply to serve as a warning to others.

JOKE

"Cash, credit, or debit?" the clerk asked after folding the sweater a woman was ready to purchase. As the customer fumbled for her wallet, the clerk couldn't help but notice a TV remote control in her purse.

"Do you always carry your TV remote?" the clerk asked.

"No," she replied. "But my husband refused to come shopping with me, so I figured looking for this would keep him busy while I was gone."

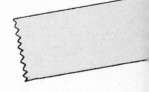

BLOOPER

Marge Gilbert is selling her almost new, queen-sized mattress. She said she has slept lightly and almost never bore down on the mattress with her full weight.

Quote

The trouble with coming right out
and letting people know where you stand
is that you become a stationary target.

JOKE

The policeman couldn't believe his eyes when he saw a woman drive past him on the freeway, busily knitting.

Quickly he pulled alongside the vehicle, rolled down his window and shouted, "Pull over!"

"No," the women yelled back cheerfully. "Socks!"

349

BLOOPER

The Tri-County Emergency Agency located in our church annex is seeking to get an unlisted phone number.

Quote

The wishbone will never replace the backbone.

JOKE

The minister and the elders called a congregational meeting to discuss emergency building repairs that needed to be fixed before winter. "We will be taking a special collection earmarked for the repairs," the minister announced. "The person who is the most generous will pick 3 hymns for next week's service."

The offering plates were passed and brought to the minister. There, on top of the pile, was a $1,000 bill. "How wonderful! Who gave this $1,000 bill?" he asked.

A little old lady in the back shyly raised her hand. "Please come up and let us thank you!" the minister urged.

When she got to the front, the minister invited her to select the hymns she wanted. Turning toward the congregation, she stretched out her arm and said, "I pick him! And him! And him!"

350

It's a Long Story . . .

A couple, who were childhood sweethearts, had married and lived in the neighborhood where they grew up. Because it was close to their 50th wedding anniversary, the couple decided to visit their old school. After a half hour reminiscing, the couple left to walk home.

Suddenly, a bag of money fell out of an armored car, landing at their feet. "Let's take it home and then contact the authorities," the wife said. At home, she counted the money: there was 5 million dollars in the bag!

"We've got to turn it in," the husband said.

"Finders keepers," his wife said greedily, promptly heading to the attic to hide the money.

The next day, two FBI men showed up at their door. "Excuse me, but did either of you find any money that fell out of an armored car yesterday?"

"No," the wife said quickly.

"She's lying!!" the husband interjected.

"Don't believe him, he's getting senile."

"Sir, start from the beginning," the agent said.

"Well," the husband began, "when we were walking home from school yesterday . . ."

The FBI agents looked at each other in alarm and said, "Let's get out of here!!"

BLOOPER

The new parochial school has an auditorium seating 1,000 people. The old auditorium only held 999.

Quote

Proud people are always letting off esteem.

JOKE

The chef at a family-run restaurant had broken her leg and came into the insurance office to file a disability claim.

As the agent scanned the claim form, he did a double take. Under "Reason unable to work," she had written: "Can't stand to cook."

352

Quote

There's nothing wrong in drinking like a fish,
providing you drink what a fish drinks.

JOKE

A woman named Gladys Dunn was new in town and
decided to visit the church closest to her apartment.

She appreciated the pretty sanctuary and the music
by the choir, but the sermon went on and on. Worse, it
wasn't very interesting. Glancing around, she saw many
people in the congregation nodding off.

Finally it was over. After the service, she turned to a still
sleepy-looking gentleman next to her, extended her hand,
and said, "I'm Gladys Dunn."

"You and me both!" he replied.

BLOOPER

The 3rd verse of "Blessed Assurance" will be sung without musical accomplishment.

Quote

Flattery is soft soap—and soap is 80 percent lye.

JOKE

A man was in the waiting room of the doctor's office when he was startled by someone loudly yelling. Listening closely, he heard, "Typhoid! Tetanus! Measles!" The man immediately went up to the receptionist and asked her what was going on.

"Oh, that," she replied. "It's just the doctor. He likes to call the shots around here."

354

BLOOPER

"The Sunday school Christmas program," explained
Superintendent Wilson, "is no longer a scared cow."

Quote

The best time for parents to put children to bed is while
they still have the strength.

JOKE

A minister was spotted in the hallway by one of the
preschool students. The youngster asked, "Do you have
an owie?"

The minister was perplexed until he realized that the
boy was staring at his clerical collar which probably
looked like a Band-Aid to him. So the minister took it off
and handed it to the little boy. On the back of the collar
tab was the manufacturer's name in embossed letters.

Seeing the boy running his fingers across the letters,
the minister asked, "Do you know what those words say?"

"Yes," said the boy, still too young to read. "Kills ticks
and fleas up to 6 months!"

355
Attention-getting Signs

On maternity ward door: Push, Push, Push.

At an optometrist's office: If you don't see what you're looking for, you've come to the right place.

On a taxidermist's window: We really know our stuff.

On a plumber's truck: We repair what your husband fixed.

Outside a tire shop: Invite us to your next blowout.

At a plastic surgeon's office: Hello, can we pick your nose?

For a towing company: We don't charge an arm and a leg. We want tows.

In a podiatrist's office: Time wounds all heels.

Posted on a residential fence: Salesmen welcome. Dog food is expensive.

On a hotel marquee: Help! We need inn-experienced people.

In a veterinarian's waiting room: Be back in 5 minutes. Sit! Stay!

356

Quote

How far a person goes these days depends on how much gas is left in the car.

JOKE

A woman was waiting for her husband's physical to be completed. When he came out, the doctor asked his wife to come into the office alone.

"Your husband is suffering from a very serious disease," the doctor said. "It's critical for you to follow these specific instructions, or your husband will die.

"Prepare 3 nutritious meals a day for him. Take care of all the chores, and don't stress him out with your problems. Most importantly, you should satisfy all of his sexual needs. In a year's time, I think your husband's health will be restored completely."

On the way home, the husband asked his wife, "What did the doctor say?"

"You're going to die," she replied.

BLOOPER

John Johnson of Farmer's Lanes in New Brunswick will offer all parishioners a discount on bowling balls—all sizes, all shapes available.

Quote

A pessimist looks at life through morose-colored glasses.

JOKE

The wedding went by without a hitch, and the handsome couple joined family and friends for more celebrating at the reception.

Sitting at the head table, the new groom began tugging at his ring. Finally he whispered to his bride, "I guess my hands swelled up or something. This ring is so tight that it's cutting off my circulation."

To which his wife replied with a smile, "That's what it's supposed to do."

BLOOPER

Wilson Gettries is offering his desk for sale. It is done in a mid-evil style.

Quote

Sincerity: to practice more than your tongue says.

JOKE

A nervous young preacher had just begun his sermon. Ten minutes into the talk, his mind went blank. Then he remembered some advice that his seminary professor had passed on for a situation like this—repeat your last point. The repetition often gets your mind back on track.

"Behold, I come quickly," he said. Nothing. He tried again, "Behold, I come quickly!" Still his mind was blank.

He tried once more, with so much oomph that he tripped and fell off the platform into the lap of a little old lady. Picking himself up, he apologized profusely.

"No, it was my fault," the woman replied. "You told me 3 times you were coming. I should have gotten out of the way."

BLOOPER

Tom Bridges has 2 cemetery plots for sale in Ridgeview Gardens. Tom said the plots can be moved, if desired.

Quote

The best way for a mother to have a few moments of peace at that end of a hectic day is to start doing the dishes.

JOKE

A lawyer parked his brand-new Lexus on the street in front of the office, ready to show it off to his colleagues. Just as he got out, a truck sideswiped the car, tearing off the driver's door.

The lawyer immediately dialed 911, and within minutes a policeman arrived. The lawyer started shouting hysterically. "My new Lexus! "

"I can't believe how materialistic you lawyers are," the cop said in disgust. "Good grief man, don't you realize that your left arm is missing? It got ripped off when the truck hit you."

"My Rolex!" screamed the lawyer.

360

I Didn't Know There Was Spellin' in Heaven . . .

A woman died and arrived at the gates of heaven. Peeking through the gates, she saw St. Peter. The woman asked, "This is such a wonderful place! How do I get in?"

"You have to spell a word," St. Peter told her.

"What word?" the woman asked.

"Love."

The woman correctly spelled *love* and she was welcomed inside.

About six months later, St. Peter asked the woman to watch the gates for him for a few minutes. While the woman was on duty, her husband arrived at the gates.

"Look who's here. I'm surprised to see you," the woman said. "How have you been?"

"Oh, I've been doing pretty well since you died," her husband said. "I married the beautiful young nurse who took care of you. And then I won the lottery. We live in a mansion and have traveled all around the world. I was water skiing when I fell, the ski hit my head, and here I am. Now, how do I get in?"

"You have to spell a word."

"What word?" her husband asked.

"Chrysanthemums."

361

BLOOPER

Tommy and Angela are renewing their vowels on Saturday. All are invited.

Quote

When one word leads to another,
it generally ends up in a quarrel,
a speech, or a dictionary.

JOKES

A boy was watching his mother open a bottle of vitamins.

"Can I open it?" he asked.

Smiling, she handed it to him. "You can try, but it is a childproof bottle." Sure enough, after numerous attempts, the little boy still hadn't opened it. Before giving it back to his mother, he turned it over and over, giving it a close inspection.

"What are you looking for?" his mother asked.

"The hidden camera," the boy said. "How else does it know that I'm a kid?"

362

BLOOPER

St. Thomas Church in Blue Ridge is looking for volunteers to help torture survivors.

Quote

Superglue is forever.

JOKE

One Christmas, a mother decided that she was no longer going to remind her children to send thank-you notes. As a result, their grandmother did not receive any acknowledgments for the generous checks she had written.

The next year things were different, however. "The children came over in person to thank me," the grandparent told her daughter triumphantly.

"How wonderful!" the mother exclaimed. "What happened?"

"This year I didn't sign the checks."

BLOOPER

Welcome all snowbirds! Here's a tip on how to enjoy your stay in Florida. To avoid alligator attack, don't swim in waters inhabited by alligators.

Quote

You can't trust dogs to watch your food.

JOKE

You need to make a New Year's resolution to *get organized*. As Benjamin Franklin so aptly put it in one of his pithy maxims: "If a man be organized, then that man be a lot more organized than the man whom do not be as organized as the first man I was talking about earlier in this maxim." Or words to that effect.

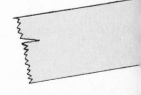

364

BLOOPER

Hymn 98—"I Heard the Bills on Christmas Day"

Quote

A good sense of humor will get you through most
problems in life. Unfortunately,
it helps mostly in retrospect.

JOKE

A husband was carrying the Christmas decorations up to
the attic for another year's storage. On one trek up the
stairs, trying to carry too many heavy boxes at once, he
slipped. Luckily, he fell only 2 steps before landing square
on his behind.

Hearing the noise, his wife yelled, "What was that
thump?"

"I just fell down the stairs," he explained.

She rushed to the staircase, "Anything broken?"

"No, no, I'm fine."

After a slight pause his loving wife said, "I meant the
ornaments."

365

Some People Are like Potatoes

* Some are very bossy and like to tell everyone what to do, but of course they don't want to dirty their hands. You might call them *Dick Taters*.

* Some never seem motivated to participate. They are content to watch while others do. They are *Speck Taters*.

* Some never do anything to help, but they are gifted at finding fault with the way others do things. They might be called *Comment Taters*.

* Some are always looking for ways to cause problems. They look for others who will agree with them. We call them *Aggie Taters*.

* Then there are those who always say they will do something, but somehow they never get around to doing anything. They are *Hezzie Taters*.

* Some put on a front and act like they are someone they are not. They are *Emma Taters*.

* Still, there *are* those who are always prepared to stop and lend a hand. They bring real sunshine into the lives of others. They definitely are *Sweet Taters*.

JIM KRAUS is a 1972 graduate of the University of Pittsburgh, with a degree in English and Communication. He attended the Paris-American Academy in France where he learned to effectively point at various menu selections as well as get lost on the Metro without even trying. Jim has been a journalist for a small-town newspaper in southern Minnesota, has worked in sales, and was an editor for a trade magazine. For the last fifteen years, he has been a senior vice-president at Tyndale House Publishers. A collector at heart, Jim is happily buried in a snowglobe collection (250) and also enjoys his 300 miniature souvenir buildings (the Statue of Liberty with an illuminated torch is his favorite). "I love collecting things that I can buy in tacky airport gift shops." Jim and his wife have written ten books together in addition to Jim's five solo efforts. The Kraus clan includes Jim, his wife, their fourth-grade son, and a sweet miniature schnauzer, Rufus, who are all allowed to coexist with their ill-tempered cat, P.D., in the Midwest.